God's Grand Design

Jesus Christ Explains How To Get Back Into Heaven

Richard Ferguson

Almighty God Speaks To All His Sacred Children

From Your Almighty Father:

"This book is written for you by my special favored son. He is my sacred child, like all of you are. But listen to what he says for I approve of His words in this book. He has worked very hard to bring you advanced truths of my creations. Richard is completely right! When he describes that the Spiritual realm and the physical universe are indeed created so all my sacred children may return to me. This will happen after the rebellion of Lucifer and the fall of Adam and Eve, as is described in your Christian Bible.

Listen to Him with both your ears for Richard has a unique and true understanding of things that are not available to those who believe in me by other means. I, your Father in Heaven, have asked Richard to do something that I have never requested any other of my children. Listen to Him for he is my messenger, and he will help lead you back to me so we may together enjoy eternal life in a paradise that each of you can barely imagine. Yet, it is waiting for you.

Richard was one of my special children even before he was born on Earth. Listening to what he has to say and reading what he has written will lead you back to me without fail. I love you so very much from the bottom of my heart. Pray for me. Ask me questions about your lives. I will answer you. Be prepared to listen to what I have to say for it will be for your eternal goodness and salvation. "

I love you so very much, Your Almighty Father

God's Grand Design

Jesus Christ Explains How To Get Back Into Heaven

Richard Ferguson

God's Grand Design: Jesus Christ Explains How To Get Back Into Heaven
by Richard Ferguson
Copyright © 2025 by Richard Ferguson
All Rights Reserved.
ISBN: 978-1-59755-845-7

Published by: ADVANTAGE BOOKS™
                 Longwood, Florida, USA
                 www.advbookstore.com

All Rights Reserved. This book and parts thereof may not be reproduced in any form, stored in a retrieval system or transmitted in any form by any means (electronic, mechanical, photocopy, recording or otherwise) without prior written copyright law, permission of the author, except as provided by United States of America.

Unless otherwise indicated, Scripture quotations taken from The Holy Bible KING JAMES VERSION (KJV), public domain.

Scriptures marked (NKJV) are taken from the Holy Bible NEW KING JAMES VERSION®. Copyright© 1982 by Thomas Nelson, Inc. Used by permission. All rights reserved.

Library of Congress Catalog Number: 2025943278

Name:	Ferguson, Richard, Author
Title:	*Jesus Christ Explains How To Get Back Into Heaven*
	Richard Ferguson
	Advantage Books, 2024
Identifiers:	ISBN: Paperback: 9781597558457
	eBook: 9781597558655
Subjects:	RELIGION: Christian Life – Inspirational

Lead Contributor and Lead Editor: Evangeline Ferguson

First Printing: July 2025
25 26 27 28 29 30 31 32   10 9 8 7 6 5 4 3 2 1

Table of Contents

ALMIGHTY GOD SPEAKS TO ALL HIS SACRED CHILDREN 2

ABOUT YOUR SACRED ANOINTED MESSENGER AND AUTHOR 9

1: INTRODUCTION 11

2: LORD JESUS AND BLESSED MOTHER MARY COMES TO ME 14

3: OUR HEAVENLY FATHER SPOKE TO ME 19

4: WHAT EXISTED BEFORE CREATION 21

5: THE DECISION TO CREATE GOD'S SACRED CHILDREN 25

6: THE FULL STORY OF CREATION WRITTEN BY OUR ALMIGHTY FATHER 28

7: GOD CREATES HIS CHILDREN IN THE SPIRIT 33

8: THE HOLY SPIRIT AND CREATION 40

9: CREATION 43

10: ALMIGHTY GOD CREATES THE PHYSICAL REALM 48

11: TIME AND DIMENSIONS 61

12: WHAT IS LIFE? WHERE DID IT COME FROM? 67

13: THE LOVING DIVINE UNITY OF ALL LIFE AND EXISTENCE 71

14: A POETIC VIEW OF GOD'S CREATIONS 75

15: THE HEAVENLY REALM 78

16: THE CHARACTER OF ALMIGHTY GOD 92

17: OUR HEAVENLY FATHER'S LOVING TEN COMMANDMENTS 102

18: IT IS ONLY THROUGH JESUS CHRIST THAT WE GO TO HEAVEN! 108

19: WHAT IS LIFE? WHERE DID LIFE COME FROM? 111

20: THE LOVING DIVINE UNITY OF ALL LIFE AND EXISTENCE 114

21: SATAN 128

22: GOD'S SACRED CHILDREN'S EXPOSURE TO SATAN & EARTH TEST...... 142

23: A CHOICE ABOUT THE EARTH TEST OR NOT 149

24: THE BEGINNING OF THE END TIMES.................................... 155

25: THE SCIENTIFIC SIDE OF WHAT OBJECTIVE REALITY IS 159

26: TO STAY IN THE KINGDOM OR NOT 168

27: SEEING MY FIRST GRANDDAUGHTER BEFORE HER BIRTH................... 177

28: HISTORICAL PERCENTAGES, WHO MAKES IT BACK INTO HEAVEN....... 180

29: COMMENTARY & OBSERVATIONS ABOUT LIVING A CHRISTIAN LIFE 211

30: CONCLUSION: 221

APPENDIX 1 222

APPENDIX 2: GOD'S SACRED CHILDREN'S HEALTH AND HEALING 235

APPENDIX 3 239

About Your Sacred Anointed Messenger and Author

Remember, please, dear Sacred child of God what is here written. I am the only Anointed Messenger of Almighty God on Earth. I have complete access to everything the Holy Trinity wishes to reveal. Everything in every book I have written is completely true in all respects because the source of all the information is directly from Almighty God Himself! I have a binding sacred covenant with our Heavenly Father about truth. Everything you will read is completely true and accurate to the very best of my ability.

Believe what our Heavenly Father said on page 2 of This Book. If not, you will look forward to the time soon after your death when Jesus Christ will look you in the eyes and ask you this question, "Why did you not believe my **Anointed Messenger?**"

Remember, please, dear Sacred child of God. I am the Anointed Messenger of Almighty God and have complete access to everything the Holy Trinity wishes to reveal. Everything in every book I have written is completely true in all respects because the source of all the information is directly from Almighty God Himself!

Believe what our Heavenly Father said on page 2 of This Book. If not, you will look forward to a time soon after your death when Jesus Christ will look you in the eyes and ask you this question, "Why did you not believe my **Anointed Messenger?**"

Richard Ferguson

1

Introduction

Everything you will read in this book is the direct words spoken to me by either a member of The Trinity or our Blessed Mother Mary. Those divine words are presented in italicized bold print. The words originating from your author are presented in normal Times New Roman text. This way, you will know who is speaking and the authority behind it. Your author is the only anointed messenger of our Heavenly Father on earth. Everything I will say is approved and inspired by Almighty God and or our Blessed Mother Mary.

This book is dedicated to answering the question everybody wonders about: "How do I get into Heaven?" Additionally, the contents of this book address many questions that people have regarding life on this earth. How do we behave on Earth so we will return to the Heavenly Kingdom? That question is answered in detail within this book. The title of this book is very revealing. It directly indicates that all of us were in the Heavenly Kingdom before we chose to come to Earth for the "Earth test. "But…yes, all of us were born in the Heavenly Kingdom before we were born into the earthly realm. We had already spent vast amounts of time with our Father before we came to Earth. The Earth test is a comprehensive observation of how you conduct your lives with all your classmates.

Those who don't wonder are blind to their loving Father's existence. This means they are in serious trouble of going to hell. What must I do to return to the Heavenly Kingdom? What rules are there for me to obey while I am on earth? It is a very good sign from a spiritual perspective if you are asking this question and attempting to understand it. It means somewhere within you, you recognize that your life has a purpose and that you are not simply a clump of cellular matter that accidentally came together through the random idea of natural selection. That is addressed herein. It indicates that you are aware of your Spiritual Self. Always remember that your Spiritual Self is eternal, while your physical self has a lifespan of only 70 to perhaps 90 years.

One thing I must mention right away is what our Heavenly Father said. I included this in the first divine book that The Trinity and I wrote together. The word "Trinity" means our almighty Father, our Lord and Savior Jesus Christ, and the Holy Spirit, who proceeds from them. The title is below. Prior to about five years ago, our Heavenly Father never once allowed His words to be written down directly. It was only after this that our Blessed Mother Mary and our Lord and Savior Jesus Christ approached me and asked me if I would become our Heavenly Father's Anointed Messenger. I said, "Yes." That is a magnificent spiritual story in and of itself.

After that, I wrote with Jesus Christ the first book in the spiritual history of mankind. To write and print and include our Heavenly Father's words into a book that is now titled" ***God's Grand Design of All Creation for Your Redemption.*** " Within human history and certainly theological history, the writing of this book is a monumental and pivotal event because it greatly expands the meanings of our beloved Holy Bible. There will be more books and booklets that have copyrighted title words in all books written from now on. Those title words are "God's Grand Design."

That first book and all the following books are written with the Divine Knowledge below: All start with what our Heavenly Father said to me, which is:

The Wonderment of Our Sacred Existence

There Is Only One Sacred Life and You Are Delightfully a Sacred Part of That

2

Lord Jesus and Blessed Mother Mary Unexpectedly Comes to Me[2]

And so, for my dear Christian friend, it is in this way that this book came into being. It is by the express desire of your **Loving Father in Heaven** that this book has been written. It is by our Lord and Savior Jesus Christ who has provided so very much of the text that is found within these pages. Yes, and it is with our Blessed Holy Mother Mary that we have provided details about the birth of our Savior Jesus Christ. If it is God speaking, ***it will always be presented as bold italicized text***. If something comes from my personal theological or scientific knowledge, or a blend of the two, then it will be normal text like this.

Something magnificent happened I never would have expected. Something God had planned for me I had no idea about. After I wrote about 20 pages about God's creation, I started seeing in the distance toward the front of me two beautiful Spiritual figures that were about perhaps 50 to 70 feet away from me. I knew they were Spiritual because, first off, I have seen Spiritual figures before. This is nothing new to me because of my past dealings with Spiritual entities. Secondly, I could see these figures with either my eyes open or closed.

The Unexpected Arrival of Jesus Christ and the Blessed Mother Mary. When I was approximately 70 years old, I was meditating after I got up and then swung my feet over the side of the bed. I noticed something very strange occurring about forty feet away in front of me. There were two spiritual entities there, just standing there and looking at me.

---

[2] God's grand design, Blessed Mother Mary speaks directly, her apparitions and the End of Times 2023

It was easy to see that one was a male with brown hair and white robes. The other person was female with blue and white robes and a blue hood over the top of her head. She was shorter than the male. The first time I saw this, having been experienced at seeing other spiritual beings, it was not that big a deal to me, but it got my attention. After a few seconds, I went about my business for the day.

The next day when I woke up, I noticed these same two spiritual people looking the same but being a little closer to me than the previous day. Well, that got my attention. Something was up but I had no idea what it was. But I had things to do, and I resumed my daily activities. Waking on the third day and swinging my feet over the right side of the bed these two spiritual people were still even closer to me than the previous night and the one before that. They remained silent, but now I knew something was up, but I did not know what. On the fourth day, they were no more than five or six feet from me in front and to my right side.

Strange, I was almost certain I knew who they were at this point. But I did not dare say anything, at least not yet, even to myself. I was now beginning to think these two spiritual people were Jesus Christ and our Blessed Mother Mary. Naw, that cannot be or so I thought. Now the fifth morning has risen. It was a morning like no other in my entire life. When I woke up lying down and staring at the ceiling, I did not see them. I wondered where they went. Soon, I was to find out in a matter of seconds. In the act of swinging my legs over the side of the bed, my eyes caught the unmistakable image of our Lord and Savior Jesus Christ and our Beloved Blessed Mother Mary.

They were silently standing right next to my right shoulder. Perhaps 4 to 6 inches away from me. This shocked the heck out of me. I did not know what to do, I did not know what to say, I did not know anything to do in any way. I was completely stunned. There I was, my feet hanging over the side of the bed with two Biblical sentient spiritual beings standing right next to me on my right side.

I started to go into a state of shock. But I had enough presence of mind to ask the following question in a telepathic way. I have used this many times before speaking with spiritual beings: I asked, "Are you who I think you are?" Jesus answered with these exact words, "**Yes, It Is I**." Instantly, I thought it strange he did not say "it is me." Because that is the incorrect English everybody uses. Proper English is exactly what Jesus said." Yes, it is I."

With that response from Jesus, everything and I mean absolutely everything within all my senses turned completely white. All my surroundings in the bedroom completely disappeared. They were gone. I no longer felt I was sitting on the edge of my bed. There was no sensation at all. The ceiling was gone, the floors were gone, and the bed I was lying on was gone. The only things that existed were my consciousness, my identity, and an awareness of who I was with and where I thought I was but apparently not anymore. Instantly, the only awareness I had was I existed, and our Lord and savior Jesus Christ and Mother Mary were close by my right side. There was nothing else. There was absolutely no fear.

The next thing I heard was dear Lord Jesus telling me to put my feet back up on the bed and just rest and remain calm as much as I could. I did that but in the process of doing it I did not see my legs anymore. I don't remember feeling them either, nor did I see the rest of the bed or the rest of the bedroom for that matter. It was just me, our loving Lord Jesus Christ, and our beloved Mother Mary. Nothing else! After an unknown time resting on the bed. Jesus told me just to keep lying down and listen to what he wanted to tell me.

He said Mother Mary and He were there to help me with the coming things our Heavenly Father wants me to do for the rest of His sacred children on earth. I do not remember His exact words but that is the central idea. Jesus also told me both He and Mother Mary would stay with me by my side forevermore. They will never leave me. I felt wonderful hearing that. After this encounter, our Lord, and Savior Jesus Christ and Our Blessed Mother Mary were indeed at my right-hand side 100% of every waking moment. I can see them in full living colors. They are with me always, and they know absolutely everything about my existence, including what I was thinking, what I was feeling, what was happening to me, and everything else directly associated with my existence. Today they remain indeed always with me by my side. There was never a moment in which I could not see them. But rather I can always see Jesus with our Blessed Mother Mary in her blue and white robes, and our Lord and savior Jesus Christ. To this day as I write this sentence, I can clearly see both standing no more than six inches from my right shoulder.

Frankly at first this whole thing was quite unnerving. But after a while I started asking Jesus a lot of questions about so many different theological topics. He is always ever so happy to answer anything I want to know. It is through this personal tutoring of our Lord Jesus I learned ever so much about creation and about all the details related to how creation works together through its individual facets of existence. Hint: All aspects of our Heavenly Father's creation work together like all the parts of a fine Swiss watch.

They mesh perfectly for one reason and one reason only. All of creation exists for the sole purpose of God's sacred children making their way back to the Heavenly Kingdom from where they came. Secondly, it is to provide His sacred children the opportunity to choose either our Father or Satan. We make this choice by how we conduct our lives. It is through the private tutoring of our Lord Jesus Christ with our Blessed Mother Mary, that gave me the most magnificent information to help all our Father's sacred children get back into heaven. Information about all of creation both in the spiritual realm and the physical realm that allowed me to write the master book "God's Grand Design of All Creation for Your Redemption." I didn't rely on any resources like online or YouTube. Why would I ever do that when Jesus Christ is the one who did indeed create the entire physical realm that we call the universe?

I just don't remember what happened after that. I must have gone into some type of temporary shock where the thought that our Lord and Savior Jesus Christ was standing right beside my right shoulder and our Blessed Mother Mary was with Him. What can I possibly say? I had no idea.

Now, I will give the people who choose not to believe in our Heavenly Father, the Holy Trinity, and our Blessed Mother the opportunity to speak and justify their lack of belief in God. Author's note: I feel very sorry for those who honestly believe that their existence is nothing more than a random chance through "random selection."

3

Our Heavenly Father Spoke to Me

August 17, 2022, 03.23 P.M.

"My dearest son Richard," you are the first that I am allowing to speak with me directly and let that be written. You are a unique child of mine, and I am very pleased."

Your Almighty Father

Yes! Our Heavenly Father speaks directly to me, his anointed Messenger on earth.

The Divine Nature of the book you are holding in your hands

This is ever so important to understand the rest of this book. Please pause for a moment and think about what this means. All the divine books I have written so far contain the exact words from our Heavenly Father, our Lord and Savior Jesus Christ, our Holy Spirit, and our Blessed Mother Mary. This is the first time in thousands of years that we have heard the words of Jesus Christ precisely as he said them to me. The same is true for our Blessed Mother Mary. Miraculous as it may seem, it is divine truth that when you read text attributed to our Heavenly Father, you are reading the exact words your Heavenly Father said to me, His Anointed Messenger. And that he has allowed to be written down. In the years ahead, these books will come to be recognized as sacred. Just not quite yet.

Yes, it can be accurately said that this book is the third one written in 2,000 years that has God's direct involvement and approval. Unlike our beloved Bible does not have the direct words of our Heavenly Father, our Lord and Savior Jesus Christ, and the Holy Spirit that proceeds from them. 66 books in our beloved Christian Bible were written by secondary sources like, for example, Jesus never wrote one thing. Each sacred book within the Christian Bible Is accurately inspired based on the words that Jesus said to the apostles and other people as he conducted his ministry in the Middle East.

However, after 2000 years, it is our beloved Almighty Father who now wants, for the first time in human history, to have his exact words published in preparation for the end of time. We have already entered the End of Times starting in 1960. <u>It is now that our Heavenly Father wants his beloved words copied down and distributed to all his sacred children on Earth</u>. Our Heavenly Father wants His exact words communicated outward to all His sacred children. This is my task, dear reader, as His Anointed Messenger.

One very important subject is about The Trinity and I want you to completely understand. This book that you are holding in your hands is a sacred book that goes beyond the Bible. But unlike biblical interpretations, which can vary from the various editions of our sacred Bible, <u>this book contains the direct words as spoken by each member of The Trinity and our Blessed Mother Mary.</u>

4

What Existed Before Creation

Question From Me: Dear Father, what existed before you created what we children know of? What was it like where you existed?

Answer: Revealed From Our Almighty God:

"Paradise perfect in every way beyond anything you can possibly understand. Yes, the three of us, your Almighty Father, me, my begotten son, and the Holy Spirit, which connects us all, proceed from us to the dimensions we are contemplating to create.

1. *We love our existence so very much that we wish to expand to include our children,*
2. *Which we want them to voluntarily love us from their hearts*
3. *Chosen by their free will.*
4. *We have free will to do what pleases us*
5. *And we want our children to inherit this as well.*
6. *The space and dimensions that we live or exist in are endless.*
7. *There are no limitations. Everything is absolute perfection.* [3]

As you described, we live in a timeless way even when it is so easy to create a timeline that, if we wish and, begins and ends at any particular point. If we wanted, we could create a timeline that you exist in, and we could observe how things develop and proceed to their ultimate fruition. We have done these many times before.

---

[3] Our Father in Heaven created us so as to expand His pleasure and fulfillment by loving His children and they love Him in return through their free will.

If we want something, all we need to do is think it into existence. [4] *Then we can do whatever we choose with it. Each of us three are infinite beings and complex beyond any kind of understanding. It gives us great pleasure and joy to interact with one another as we can explore each other in such intimate and joyful ways. To see all the differences and experience all the different endless facets of our personalities and characters. Our interaction and exploration of one another can be endless if we choose. What joy, fulfillment, happiness, and ecstasy we experience by doing this together. We have no need for anything else, but the Triad published three.* [5]

Question: Why Did You Create us, your sacred children in your image?

Answer: At some timeless point, we collectively decided that we wanted to create an additional source of pleasure and enjoyment, and love for all three of us. We thought into existence the idea of our children, our sacred children, whom we love so dearly as we love one another. We bestowed upon our children limited talents but enough for them, you, to thrive in the physical realm we have not yet created. We know you will need this because we already know that one of our future angels will rebel and then hate our children, trying his best to destroy what we lovingly created. Our children are part of us.

This is why there is so much evil in your physical world. This is why we created the physical world, because we must go into it; the law of degradation is what your scientists call entropy. Nothing in this world, including your physical bodies that we thought into existence, will be able to exist forever as we do. There will come a point when all those with free will that we bestowed upon all our children will become a fork in the path. Where some of you will choose to love your Father, His

---

[4] Nothing is impossible for Almighty God

[5] Each being of The Trinity that is Almighty God is infinitely complex and joyful for the other two to explore and enjoy.

begotten son, me, and the Holy Spirit that binds everything together in glorious love and ecstasy.

We already know of each of you who has chosen to be with your creator in the perfect paradise we have already created. The others that have rejected us, we are so sorrowful about what all they will go the way of entropy and dissolve ultimately into nothingness. This is the only kind of pain we have in our hearts, but the rebellion of Lucifer with his pride is what created all this pain and suffering. He will go the way of entropy and ultimately dissolve into nothingness from whence he came. [6]

On your time, to mention, it is getting short. And our begotten son will return to the physical realm and separate those destined for an existence of perfect ecstasy from those who will ultimately dissolve as your universe will. I cannot express to your limited senses just how much we three love you with all our hearts. That is such a limited way of saying what we really feel for each of you, our children, who chose to be with us into eternity, which will never end. We love you so very much, my son. We look forward to greeting you and your permanent home with all those that you love, and, yes, my son, including your doggies that you love so much. [7] *I hope this answers your question about our existence before we started to create different realms to make your existence possible with us in a timeless paradise.* [8]

I love you, ." Your Almighty Father

Never in my life have I heard such powerful words spoken to me. I find it remarkably beautiful that our Heavenly Father even knows how much

---

[6] Astronomers, astrophysicists, and cosmologists are concluding that our universe due to dark energy will expand without end and result in nothingness. This is a mainstream hypothesis.

[7] God knows and understands each of us in magnificent detail. He even knows about my love for my dogs.

[8] God loves us so very much that if He did not create the Spiritual realm and importantly the physical realm, we would not be able to be redeemed from sin and not be able to join The Trinity in their timeless realm of infinite joy and fulfillment. More on this later.

I love my little doggies. On another occasion, he told me how to play with them in heaven and have as many doggies as I wish. This makes my spine tingle with joy and love. Our Almighty Father did indeed answer all my questions about the existence of The Trinity before they started to create realms that would be needed to save us, his children, from sin.

He explained precisely why they created the different realms I will describe in the following pages. God loved his sacred children so much that not only did he send his only begotten son, [9]but he also created multiple realms that would be needed for our salvation on an individual basis. Yes, God loves us! So much he created us in his image and created this universe we live in so we can decide through our belief in Him and loving actions to join Him in an eternal loving paradise. He also created other realms designed to support our lives on this physical earth to make it possible for us to choose our Almighty Father so we can live with Him in paradise for eternity.

So, dear reader, remember this. The entire universe we live in, the stars, and everything within it has been specifically designed and fine-tuned for us and only us to receive redemption from sin if we choose through our free will. It is for this reason that the entire universe exists. Think of that, dear reader, and think about how precious you are to Almighty God if He would do all of this for your individual redemption.

---

[9] John 3:16 NKJV

5

The Decision to Create God's Sacred Children

Creating God's Sacred Children / A Personal Discussion

I know that all your sacred children are like everything else created by yourself and your unlimited love and power. When was it, dear Father, that the Holy Trinity decided to create us, all your children, and why did you choose to do this?

Our Heavenly Father
July 1, 2022

"Yes, my beloved son, you most certainly are. I love you ever so much. You are exceptional in our eyes. It gives me great joy and delight to tell you these things about us. Your interest in The Trinity gives us delight and joy, and when your book is done, you, too, will receive joy with what you have written. Your question is about, for now, how you and the rest of God's children were created. I will answer that.

This was eons ago. <u>I paused for a moment for your mind to catch up with me. Are you ready now?</u>

(Dear reader, please make a special mental note about what our Heavenly Father just spoke to me in writing this book. It clearly states that our Almighty Father knows where my mind is at. He also knows where your mind is at and everyone else <u>all the time</u>! This is very normal within the spiritual realm because there are no secrets. Our Heavenly Father knows precisely what is going on inside our heads. As I stated earlier within this book, all of us sacred children of our Heavenly Father are unique expressions of our Father Himself, and we are inseparable unless we decide to reject our loving Father. People who do that sentence themselves to hell and permanent separation from our loving Trinity and the Heavenly Kingdom. That simple sentence above contains and reveals a magnificent, loving truth of our human existence.)

<u>A Special Note</u>: To all the crooks and dishonest people on earth, your Heavenly Father and the rest of The Trinity know absolutely every stinking and crooked thought you have ever had in your head.

Yes, dear Father, thank you. ***Previously, The Trinity had decided that we wanted children who would reflect our beauty and some of the characteristics that we have between us. We wanted our children to have free will as we do. We wanted them to have a limited number of powers we must prepare them for one day they would join us in the dimensions we occupy. They would then be able to experience some of the joys and ecstasy that we experience and enjoy in our lives.***

They will be able to experience this with us. It is beyond your understanding what we can do, what we can experience, and the pure ecstasy and depth of love that we can experience by being who we are. But we have given you as our children the capability to reach magnificent heights that our children can reach if you develop the capabilities, we have already given you. The experiential part of being us is something that you cannot understand. And for now, you cannot understand the experiential part of what you can become. Still, you can achieve a wonderfully delicious and magnificent joyful existence that a few of your religious traditions have only hinted at.

To all of God's sacred children.

My dear son Richard is bringing you this message to my will. So, you can understand us more deeply and very much. The Trinity today loves you so very much, so very deeply, as we extend our arms to every one of you and love, complete love, and acceptance. We pray that you, every one of you, accept our offer of peace and acceptance to pray on your knees and accept us as your God of peace and love. So that there will never again be one act of violence or selfishness in any way from this moment on.

Resist any person who advocates in any way any act of hatred, selfishness, or division. Surely, they will lead you to hell, and ultimately, you will be dissolved into nothingness. Richard is my messenger to you. Listen to Him well, for he will lead you to me. I will go now. There will be further messages in this book.

From God your Father, in His name, I love you. Amen."

Designing God's Sacred Children

The following text is exactly what God Almighty revealed to me. There are a few spots where some sentences have extra words that do not make sense, but I included them for completeness' sake. One thing we need to be sensitive to is time. Here in the physical real world, our time proceeds at a much different pace than in the Heavenly Kingdom.

So, depending on the desire of Almighty God, a day could seem like a thousand years here on earth. It is undetermined as to how long it took The Trinity to design our human bodies. Yet Almighty God does say, "It took us a very long time." It is exceedingly interesting that <u>our Godly designed bodies have been uniquely designed to be interfaced to BOTH the physical realm and the Spiritual realm equally well with ease.</u>

This is a necessity so we can carry out our mission of deciding which road to take while we are on earth for all eternity; our choice is obvious for us, dear children of God. The Heavenly Road with Almighty God or the Satanic Road to hell and obliteration into nothingness. God created/thought us, His children, into existence before the physical realm was created. We all dwelled with The Trinity in The Heavenly Kingdom with God our Father for a delightfully long period. Where else would we be when you think about it? Of course, we all wanted to be with our parents that loved us more than can be described.

6

The Full Story of Creation Written by Our Almighty Father

Our Heavenly Father
August 3, 2022

Note: What you are about to read is the <u>only place in all of existence</u> that is written directly by our Almighty Father. It describes in detail the creation of the different realms of existence. Everything here benefits our Father's sacred children on earth. It is only within the series of books with the headline, "God's <u>Grand Design</u>." You will find this exquisite and loving sacred literature nowhere else in the universe.

"It took us a very long time to design the features and characteristics of our sacred children. We knew they would be crafted in our image. What does that mean? It means that they would have some of the capabilities that we have. It does not mean that they would look like us because we are formless and are something that has no boundaries that you can define. Yet for our children, you would need to have boundaries because for us to interface with you, you would need to live in the physical world that we have not created yet.

We would need to create a physical world that you would live in, but also interface with the Spiritual realm where we could communicate with you. So, we would have to create a being that was physical in nature and could survive in a physical realm that could also thrive in a physical environment. But this being should also be able to communicate with us. And with their creator, so that we can give our sacred children the opportunity to choose. To choose whether they wanted to through their free will, join us in the Heavenly realm or choose the sinful realm after the coming rebellion by Lucifer.

We already know that Lucifer will rebel against us and through His hatred he will attack our children and tempt all our children to follow Him. <u>*We know that most of our children will be fooled and follow Him into hell where ultimately, they will be dissolved into nothingness.*</u> *They will go the way of entropy run wild in the physical realm. Those who choose, through their free will and love for us there create or to love us will join us in an unimaginably beautiful and loving paradise. A paradise that they will live with us forever, eternally, with no end.*

We needed to design a physical body. One that had two fundamental characteristics. Primarily one that could withstand the biological requirements to remain healthy for a relatively long period of time. Such that they could grow and prosper with sufficient time. Since there will be time, the dimension of time, to learn about our existence. And decide whether they want to follow us through their free will and love to accept us or not and demonstrate that in this physical realm and that will be recorded throughout all history.

Or if they reject our offer of love and decide to follow Satan instead, in which case, they will choose the path of obliteration and ultimately dissolve into nothingness. They will be using their free will to determine this. Their bodies must also be able to reproduce to bring on new generations until our Almighty Father chooses to bring me back in my second coming.

This brings on a whole host of biological challenges for us; this is what makes us the most amount of time to design. We chose the path, the only path, of something you call DNA and RNA. <u>*It is incredibly complex, and your scientists have come a long way to get to understanding its intimate complexity. Some of your scientists have foolishly said that what we designed accidentally occurred. We still laugh about that.*</u> *Some of your scientists have observed that the whole universe of yours was created by us. So carefully that it was indeed* *designed to in some cases to one part in 10 to the 140th power of delicate design so that the earth could support human life.* [10]

They are correct. Now, back to designing life. We had to create the human body so it could fend for itself with features of a planet that could sustain itself for billions of years, and we did so on the planet called Earth. There is no other planet in your universe that is like the one where you are at now.

There will come a time not too long from now when it will not be possible for Earth to support life any longer. Look around you at your sister planets even they cannot support life like on earth. There are reasons for that. [11] *The first human beings we set up on the earth had a full complement of chromosomes and were able to reproduce with a female that we also put on the earth. Your story of Adam and Eve is close to the truth. They did not come out of the swamp as the fairytale that the Abiogenesis people like to promote. It happened at our will. We lovingly put them there in a most beautiful place surrounded by much food, delicious trees, and a stream to support human life, and then we woke them up, male and female.*

And things proceeded from there. It did take us what you would call a long time to design the cyclical helix that is self-reproducible within the cells of the human body. But yes, we did design that through our thoughts; it was a collective effort of the triad. It is a beautiful work of art, and we are proud of what we do for our children. They are sacred to us, and we plan to have every child of ours be a full member of the

---

[10] Dear Dr. Hugh Ross: I dedicate this section to all your hard work proving how God created the universe

[11] Scientists in the field of astrophysics, astronomy and cosmology in the last 20 years have come to understand that the earth has enjoyed a Goldilocks cycle that has supported life for the last billion years or so. But that cycle is coming to an end very shortly. It will become quickly harder and harder to support life on our planet as it does today. Dr. Hugh Ross and others have published books on this topic like The Improbable Planet

Kingdom. All they must do is say yes to our offer of love, and then they will be members of the Holy Kingdom with paradise forever eternal."

Our plan was straightforward. After we woke them, the male and the female became the stewards of the garden. Which was full of delicious food of many different kinds that would completely nourish the needs of the male and female and all their children. This is the Adam and Eve that is in your Bible. We also knew at some point; Lucifer would appear to them and tempt them away from our sacred plan. Where they would multiply upon the earth, grow and become fruitful in and of themselves, and fill the land with their descendants many times over. They would never feel pain or destruction, for they were our children. Such things as pain would remain unknown to them. Pain is something that is unknown to the children of God.

However, Lucifer grew in his hatred of Almighty God to the point where he could not stand himself any longer. And he became consumed with his hatred of God's children who were made in His image and became so obsessed with destroying God's pure and perfect children on earth. As you know, God gave all His children the gift of free will. This is because before we created our children, we wanted each of them to love us voluntarily. And choose us freely because of their free will to love us freely and not be forced in any way.

This is the only way. It cannot be otherwise. What good is the love of a robot?

Lucifer took on the form of a beautiful animal that lived in the trees. It could speak beautifully, and its breath was succulent and soft. It was beguiling to behold. It lived in many different trees. But there was one tree that both male and female were told that they should never eat of its fruit; it was the tree of the knowledge of good and evil.

Eating that tree would give the male and female the knowledge they should never know. It would wipe away their pure innocence and they would be pure no more. They would become tainted creatures that could now see the manner of sinful ways and could never return to their purity *of Almighty God. From that moment, God not only would the male and female be impure, but the seed of the male would transmit their impurity throughout all the generations to follow, and it would never stop. It would now take an act of blood sacrifice of God Himself to redeem what Satan has brought to God's children. That would not come until many generations have come and gone. Lastly, pain and suffering have entered the world, and they stay there with mankind until the end of time.*

7

God Creates His Children in The Spirit

My dear fellow Christians, it is indeed with great joy I have the immense honor from our Heavenly Father to bring to you The Trinity's most profound thoughts about all creation and their sacred children. This next section discusses the creation of us as Spiritual, sacred and holy children of our loving Father in Heaven. I know you will find a few things attached to this topic that I know you will find revealing and sometimes humorous due to my observations of what I see in the Heavenly realm.

Jesus Christ
2023

"Yes, my son, God did first create all His children in the blink of an eye. From your time perspective, it took quite a while, but from our time perspective, it was indeed a blink of an eye. Remember your Heavenly Father lives in so many different dimensions all at the same time. He created all His children in Spiritual form first. Each one of them was completely different in mind and in Spiritual body. Each one had different talents, different aspirations, different everything.

They all look the same if you gaze upon them from the outside. Previously, he said they looked like white bowling pins, and yes, laughably, you are right. And their eyes did indeed look like tiny black dots with their nose stuck in the middle. I laughed the first time I heard you say that because that's precisely what they look like. My dear son, you do have a wonderful sense of humor. That is one of the things I certainly love about you.

Our Heavenly Father wanted to enjoy their existence for a very long period in the Heavenly Kingdom before he provided them with a physical body. So, they would be able to choose whether they would stay with Him in the Heavenl because he did indeed give them all free will as the three of us have free will. This is very important because God has His infinite love and free will and will never force anything upon anyone under any circumstance which includes all His beloved children. I will rest for now because I've got way ahead of you.

(Author's Note: This was always a problem for me when I was receiving sacred thoughts from our Almighty Father, our Lord and Savior Jesus Christ, and, to a lesser degree, our beloved and Blessed Mother Mary. To them, I must feel like a glacier moving at 8 cm per year trying to keep up with their thoughts, which I know are a zillion times faster than me. This is a good example of being in multiple timelines.)

Again, as a reminder, your Father in Heaven knew from the beginning one of His angels, Lucifer, would rebel against Him, attack all His beloved children, and succeed to a considerable degree. And then turning most of His children against Him in the physical world. This would be a very heart-wrenching and heartbreaking experience for your loving Father in Heaven. But your beloved Father felt it was worth it because the remaining children would be choosing your Father to love Him for all eternity through their free will. They would adore Him entirely through the love in their hearts, which would give all three of us such enormous joy; it's something we've never experienced before, and we look forward to with heartfelt thanks.

So, all of God's children spent an astounding, enormous, and uncountable amount of time with the three of us in the Heavenly Kingdom. This is before they started to be born into both the Spiritual and physical realms, which your Heavenly Father did co-create simultaneously. The Spiritual realm and the physical realm depend upon each other just as the physical bodies of His children do. One relies upon the other just as the brains of His children are split into two pieces where one amplifies the Spirit, and one amplifies the physical. In this manner, your loving Almighty Father is ever so close to each one of His children that he loves so very much."

Question: What was life like for God's children in the Heavenly Kingdom before they were born to earth?

"During this time when God's children were all Spiritual beings, there were no limits. They could think of something, and to some degree, it would appear before their tiny black eyes and behold. There it was, they would play with the things they created, and they would enjoy each other immensely. And they would cooperate with each other, and they would love each other enormously, the cooperation between each other was a joy to behold. There was no male, and there was no female.

For that, they would have to wait until they were born into the physical world. Oh, they had such a wonderful time they could go from here to there just by thinking about it. They had no limits. There were oceans. There were mountains, there were deserts. There was nothing you could imagine, and they couldn't get hurt. They could play hide and seek as you could imagine, and they invented different games as children do. Their loving Father took all of this in with great joy and happiness and delight in absolutely everything he saw. And so did the other two of us as well. The wonderment of children is so contagious, and the joy abounded beyond anything we imagined.

For a fleeting moment, we in The Trinity thought perhaps we could let things stay as they were. But we knew we couldn't keep our children in a bottle because we had given them free will and imagination as well. So, sooner or later, we knew that they would become restless within any dimension of time, and that is something we cannot bring upon our beautiful children. So, it was then that your Almighty Father in Heaven created both the Spiritual and physical realms together. They are intended to work together because, as you have said before, our children's physical body is made of two parts: a physical and a Spiritual part. More on this in detail later. My dearest son, Richard, I love you so very much I want to thank you for writing this book so my words can be spread to many others of my children. Your blessings will be great.

Amen."

The Very Core of God's Sacred Children

Question: Dear Lord, I know all of us, children of God, were created as Spiritual beings. You said earlier that we spent numerous eons of time in the Heavenly Kingdom with our Father, with you and the Holy Spirit. This time was magnificent, filled with joy, fulfillment, and learning about ourselves and creation. Lucifer's rebellion happened long before our creation. The Trinity, working together, created all that is seen and unseen for us children to have a pathway back to the Heavenly Kingdom.

My question is based on this: were we, God's sacred children, compelled to be born on this earth for our redemption after the fall of Adam and Eve? Were we given a choice by our Father to stay in the Kingdom?

"My dearest son, you have asked a marvelous question. As you know, after you were created, you were given the same gift of free will. The free will your Father also bestowed upon all His angels and the love between all the individuals that are part of all of God's creation. This also applies, my dear son, to creations that are beyond the ones that you know of. There are more.

The situation before the Earth was habitable in its galactic development was that you and all of God's sacred children were such a loving and utterly endearing part of the Heavenly Kingdom. All of you were completely sinless. I must emphasize that all of you were incapable of any sin even though you possessed the wonderful gift of free will. However, when Satan rebelled against your Heavenly Father, everything changed. This event caused the potential for God's sacred children to also fall away from us in the Holy Trinity. This rebellion happened long before your Father created all of you, Adam and Eve, and so on.

Life As God's Sacred Child!

My dear sacred children of Almighty God, this section is to describe who we are as sacred children of our Father. Why we are created. Why we have the spiritual gifts we do, like the most powerful one. Which is free will, why we live on the earth, the nature of the Heavenly Kingdom as compared to the nature of the Earth after Satan invaded it with all his hatred and demons.

My dear fellow Christians, it is indeed with magnificent joy that I have the immense honor from our Heavenly Father to bring to you The Trinity's most profound thoughts. Thoughts about all creation and their sacred children. This next section discusses the creation of us as spiritual, sacred children of our loving Father in Heaven. There are several things attached to this topic that I know you will find revealing and sometimes humorous due to my observations of what I see in the Spiritual Realm Heavenly realm.

Question: Are there any other details that you would like to share with your sacred children about our creation and subsequent Earth test?

Jesus Christ
2024

"Yes, my son, God did first create all His children in the blink of an eye. From your time perspective, it took quite a while, but from our time perspective, it was indeed a blink of an eye. Remember your Heavenly Father lives in so many different dimensions all at the same time. He created all His children in Spiritual form first. Each one of them was completely different in mind and in Spiritual body. Each one had different talents, different aspirations, different everything.

They all look the same if you were to gaze upon them from the outside. Previously, you said they looked like white bowling pins, and yes, laughably, you are right. And their eyes did indeed look like small black dots with their nose stuck in the middle. I laughed the first time I heard you say that because that's precisely what they look like. My dear son you do have a wonderful sense of humor. That is one of the things I certainly love about you.

Our Heavenly Father wanted to enjoy their existence for a long period of time in Heaven before he provided them with a physical body. So, they would be able to choose whether they would stay with Him in the Heavenly Kingdom. Because he did indeed give them all free will as the three of us have free will. This is very important because God has His infinite love and free will and will never force anything upon anyone under any circumstance which includes all His beloved children.

I will rest for now because I've got way ahead of you.

(This was always a problem for me when I was receiving sacred thoughts from our Almighty Father, our Lord and Savior Jesus Christ, and, to a lesser degree, our beloved and Blessed Mother Mary. To them, I must feel like a glacier moving at 8 cm per year, trying to keep up with their thoughts, which I know are a zillion times faster than mine. This is a good example of being in multiple timelines.)

Again, as a reminder, your Father in Heaven knew from the beginning one of His angels, Lucifer, would rebel against Him. And would attack all His beloved children and would succeed to a very large degree and turn most of His children against Him in the physical world. This would be a very heart wrenching and heartbreaking experience for your loving Father in Heaven.

But your beloved Father felt it was worth it because the remaining children would be choosing your Father to love Him for all eternity through their free will. They would adore Him completely through their love in their hearts. And that would give all three of us such enormous joy that it is something we have never experienced before, and it is something that we look forward to with heartfelt thanks.

So. all of God's children spent a wonderful enormous and uncountable amount of time with the three of us in the Heavenly Kingdom. Before they started to be born into both the Spiritual and physical realms which your Heavenly Father did co-create simultaneously. The Spiritual realm and the physical realm depend upon each other just as the physical bodies of His children do. One relies upon the other just as the brains of His children are split into two pieces where one amplifies the Spirit, and one amplifies the physical. In this manner your loving Almighty Father is ever so close to each one of His children that he loves so very much."

Question: What was life like for God's children in the Heavenly Kingdom before they were born to earth?

"During this time when God's children were all Spiritual beings, there were no limits. They could think of something, and to some degree, it would appear before their very tiny black eyes. And behold, there it was, they would play with things they created, and they would enjoy each other immensely. And they would cooperate with each other, and they would love each other enormously, the cooperation between each other was a joy to behold.

There was no male, and there was no female. For that, they would have to wait until they were born into the physical world. Oh, they had such a wonderful time they could go from here to there just by thinking about it. They had no limits. There were oceans. There were mountains, there were deserts. There wasn't anything you couldn't possibly imagine. And it was impossible for any of our Father's sacred children to get hurt. They could play hide and seek as you could imagine, and they invented different games as children do. Their loving Father took all of this in with great joy and happiness and delight in absolutely everything he saw. And so did the other two of us as well. The wonderment of children is so contagious, and the joy abounded beyond anything we imagined.

For a fleeting moment, we in The Trinity thought perhaps we could let things stay as they were. But we knew we couldn't keep our children in a bottle, for we had also given them free will and imagination. So, sooner or later, we knew that they would become restless within any dimension of time, and that is something we cannot bring upon our beautiful children. So, it was then that your Almighty Father in Heaven created both the Spiritual and physical realms together. They are intended to work together because, as you have said before, our children's physical body is made of two parts: a physical and a Spiritual part. More on this in detail later.

My dearest son, Richard, I love you so very much I want to thank you for writing this book so my words can be spread to many others of my children. Your blessings will be great. Jesus Christ. Amen."

8

The Holy Spirit and Creation

Within the Bible and other biblical literature, when it comes to the topic of creation, we attribute it to Almighty God. This is completely correct. For Almighty God has created everything seen and unseen. However, as Christians, we must continue to remember that our Father in Heaven is also described as a Trinity of three members, each of whom is infinite and all-powerful. This means all three persons within The Trinity were directly involved in the creation of the Spiritual realm and the physical realm that we call the universe.

Earlier in this book, I described in detail the attributes of the members within The Trinity and how they explored and created things together, exploring each other's infinite character to their magnificent joy and fulfillment.

But the Holy Spirit, which proceeds from Almighty God, also had a direct role in creating all the realms of existence that we, God's children, are aware of. This is something that we need not forget. Regarding our Holy Spirit, he played a vital role in the creation of the Spiritual realm, the physical realm, and us God's children.

Revealed by our Almighty Father.
August 9, 2022, 7:55 AM

"Our Holy Spirit was indeed intimately involved with the creation of what is said above. He brought to our creation a sense of equity and fairness that our children will learn from within their experience in the physical realm. Everything in creation is in perfect balance and harmony. Remember, all of creation, every particle of it, was created out of complete nothingness.

It is your Holy Spirit, our Holy Spirit, that proceeded from the true entity to ensure that all creation was in equilibrium. This is a form of fairness. And it also brings forth that when

something occurs either naturally or man-made, feedback from a violation of equality immediately presents itself. And forces of the universe act upon it to bring it back into the balance and equity that your Father in Heaven has commanded.

All the Structures we take for granted

The Holy Spirit has created the organizing forces and structures that hold all things together that have been created by our Father in Heaven. It is these forces that again have created balance and equilibrium that you, as our children, never even think about. And that is okay because your Father in Heaven has provided this for you through the Holy Spirit. So, you may participate in walking up the pathway toward the Heavenly realm and live forever, eternally, with us in The Trinity. And, most notably, your Father, your Almighty Father, in Heaven and in a paradise that exceeds by far anything your mind can imagine.

Out of nothingness, my dear son, the forces of balance, equity, fairness, and equilibrium have been created by your Father in Heaven within the auspices of our Holy Spirit.

It is also true that when each of our children is born into the physical realm on earth, they are born with a sense of fairness and equality. When a very small child interacts with another, if the other violates this fairness by taking away a toy, there is an instant reaction to this disequilibrium incident. And the concept of ownership that is inborn within our children comes into play. When the child loses their toy, immediately retrieve that to restore the previous balance. This kind of thing is a magnificent force that applies to all creations, seen and unseen.

When the planets revolve around the sun in predictable orbits, it is an equilibrium. This did not happen by chance. Instead, it happened by design. Some people call this Mother Nature working. This is a primitive way of saying and recognizing the balancing of all things seen and unseen within all creation. Every phenomenon always seeks balance in one way or another. It is what mankind's laws are all about at its root. My dear son, I hope this answers your question about our Holy Spirit and its primary role in the creation of all that is seen and unseen. Lastly, there is more that the Holy Spirit has done that you will not understand. I love you."

I hope the above will reveal some of the details and the Almighty power that the Holy Spirit possesses within The Trinity to benefit us, God's children. Remember that everything within existence, with all its laws, forces, and attractions in creation, has come from nothingness. Without nothingness, it means that even the slightest shred of the concept of balance and equilibrium does not exist at all.

Regarding nothingness, this is something that our human minds cannot fully grasp. Nothingness means the absence of anything at all. Most people associate nothingness with blackness. It is not, for blackness in and of itself is something. Therefore, it cannot be nothingness. There is no dimensionality about nothingness. There is not the slightest particle of existence within nothingness, for that would be something. Our sciences have produced the wonderment of information and better lives for God's children. However, science can never fully comprehend what nothingness is.

I hope this gives you a flavor and some insight. That in some way approaches the idea of nothingness, for nothingness is what all existence came from due to the love and action of our Holy Father in Heaven. All existence that surrounds us in any way has been created by our Almighty Father in Heaven with the other members of The Trinity. If not, there would be nothingness.

9

Creation

A Chronology of Events

I bring you the following information about creation and how it happens to put into context the next section of this book, where the details of how to get back into heaven are discussed.

Chronology of events is understood in relation to the passage of time within both the Spiritual realm and the physical realm that we, as God's sacred children, would experience.

1. God exists eternally outside of time, a timeless time, across many multiple dimensions, far more than we are aware of and can understand. The Trinity was, is and always will be existing outside of time and the physical and Spiritual worlds that are yet to come. Before the creation that we know of that we call creation of the beginning.

2. The creation of the Angels occurred an immeasurable number of eons prior to the decision to create His sacred children. They exist inside the Heavenly Kingdom in order to serve Almighty God. More angels will be created by our Heavenly Father to serve His purposes in the larger Spiritual realm. And His sacred children going forward after they are created and spend eons of time with Almighty God in the Heavenly Kingdom. Angels will also be assigned to protect our Heavenly Father's sacred children when the time comes after our creation.

3. Upon deciding to create His sacred children made in His image, God prepared the way for His children by creating many more angels to serve as messengers and more between His children and Himself. They will also serve as guardian angels to protect His sacred children from the yet-to-come Satan and His demons.

4. Eons before The Trinity thought of creating children in their image, God certainly already knew of Lucifer's plan to rebel against Him. Remember our Almighty Father exists across all time, from the alpha to the omega. So, in addition to creating more angels to serve His yet-to-be-created children, God also created both the increased spiritual realm and the physical realm that will contain the earth. It is the earth that will host His sacred children where they are to decide where they want to spend eternity. Will it be with our Almighty Father or with Satan and his demons?

5. Always remember this: For those who choose to spend their eternity in God's loving paradise, they will indeed be overwhelmed with the beauty and the intense feelings of love and understanding within their hearts. Life within the Heavenly Kingdom is a paradise beyond any human mind.

The Heavenly Kingdom is reserved for only those who have lived on Earth where they obeyed the will of our Heavenly Father. Where they obeyed the 10 Commandments and the three Rules of life that are explained within this book. Each sacred child of our Heavenly Father chooses whether it is heaven or hell for their eternal destiny. Surprisingly, it is NOT God that sends people to hell. Every one of God's sacred children is in complete control of their destiny, and they make their choice of Heaven or hell. The very nature in which they conduct their lives on this earth is the determinative factor in whether a child of God goes to Heaven or hell. It will be the sacred child of God that determines whether it will be heaven or hell. Refer to another section of this book where I explain in detail the "Earth Test."

This is where God created our universe and all the physical and Spiritual laws that surrounded it. The same is true for the Spiritual realm. Both realms are created tailor-made to perfection to match the needs of us sacred children while we are here on earth. The Spiritual realm matches are interior Spirit and minds so we can communicate with the divine. The physical realm matches perfectly with the needs of our bodies so we may live on the earth long enough to decide our eternal destiny. The choice is very simple, choose our Heavenly Father by living our lives according to His laws or choose Satan and Hell by rejecting our Father and demonstrating that by living sinful lives.

Said differently, God creates it in anticipation of the dual nature of His now-existing sacred Spiritual children. They will have physical bodies to procreate across the ages allowing more and more of His sacred Spiritual children the opportunity to live with Him for all eternity in paradise. Now, Almighty God also has a place to send Lucifer after His coming unsuccessful rebellion along with one-third of the angelic realm.

6. It is then that Lucifer falls in love with Himself, and through pride and arrogance, he attempts to seize God's rightful throne. War begins in Heaven, and Lucifer becomes Satan, the adversary. And he is thrown down to the pre-existing Spiritual realm outside of the Heavenly Kingdom and to the physical realm, where he becomes the prince of Earth. In human time, the war between Almighty God and Lucifer with His cadre of fallen angels concludes within a blink of an eye. Lucifer never had any chance and is thrown out of the Heavenly Kingdom.

7. It was some undetermined time later after the expulsion of Lucifer and His angels," out of the Heavenly Kingdom that our Father creates you and me. Almighty God our Father creates all His sacred Spiritual children made in His image within the blink of an eye. We reside within the Heavenly Kingdom and live and play with our Almighty Father in the Kingdom for more eons of time as we know it. It is here His children learn so much about their loving Father's characteristics and plans. It is a magnificent and Holy time of joy, love, and fulfillment for everyone.

8. As part of the Spiritual realm, Almighty God creates a special place that is sealed off from the rest of the Spiritual realm. It is this place that will have ties to the physical realm, the purpose of which will become obvious at the End of Times. This is the place that Satan and

His demons will govern. They will govern over all of God's children who purposely rejected God during their human life on earth. At this point, everything is now prepared for the coming rebellion of Lucifer and one-third of the angelic host.

9. It is some long undetermined time after this instantaneous war that God's children begin to be born into the physical realm. The physical universe and the planet Earth are now ready to receive and support the physical bodies of God's sacred children. We arrive on earth in a pure state of love intimately connected to their creator. They walk and talk with Almighty God within the perfect garden of what we call Eden. Firstborn into the physical world is the male named Adam. Later his companion was fashioned out of Adam's body, called female, and named Eve. Scholars say this was about 3,000 BC.

10. Satan appears to the naïve Eve as a wise serpent and lies to her. He lies that they would become like God if they ate the fruit from the tree of the knowledge of good and evil. Eating from this tree was explicitly forbidden by Almighty God. Both Adam and Eve blatantly disobey their Father by eating from the forbidden tree of the knowledge of good and evil. Because of this, they were thrown out of the garden where life was so excellent as intended by God.

11. From that point onward, all mankind becomes separated from Almighty God and must now grovel in the dirt to sustain themselves and all their future children. From this point onward, the Christian Bible and associated Biblical literature describe in detail what happens next. This including the offer of redemption made possible

by the painful sacrifice and death of God's only begotten son, Jesus Christ. It is only after our Lord and Savior's sacrifice and ascension into Heaven that we, God's sacred children, can say yes to God's offer of eternal life in paradise with Him.

12. From this point on all of God's sacred children that come to the physical realm on earth now participate in Spiritual warfare. We Christians must fight against the completely hateful group of demons led by princes and principalities of the Satanic realm. All the hate-filled destruction on earth emanates from the sealed-off part of the Spiritual realm called hell. To clarify, Satan and his demons are Spiritual beings, and they have some access remaining into the general Spiritual realm. They use this to destroy whatever they can that is created by God. This allows them to deceive as many of God's sacred children as they can. Once a child of God thoroughly rejects our Almighty Father with their lives and their physical death, they will go to hell prepared by our Heavenly Father for those who do so.

13. Remember that there are only two fundamental moral and ethical forces within all creation. The pure and perfect Love of our God or the Hate in all its forms directly from Satan. There are no other fundamental moral and ethical forces. It is one or the other.

14. This leads us in summary to the situation we have today on earth. However, keep in mind that this evil and painful situation on earth will not last for much longer. Almighty God will bring the physical earth to a close in the not-too-distant future. Also, our Lord and Savior Jesus Christ will return to this earth to establish love and peace among all that dwell here. With this, I will end this extremely shortened history.

10

Almighty God Creates the Physical Realm

Why God Created This Physical Universe:

What a magnificent story of God's love for His future creations (yes, more than we know about) and how He thoughtfully prepared everything to such fantastic precision for the benefit of His children. This is the magnificent and tremendous love story of a Father to His children. It is indeed a love story of our Almighty and loving Father. He wished, with the other two members of The Trinity, to expand their personal enjoyment and fulfillment by having sacred children who would love them through their own free will.

Their choice to love our Heavenly Father must be through His children's free will. For Almighty God will not force anyone into something they do not choose. If anything, if it is forced, it cannot be true love. God is the essence of love. To love our Heavenly Father must be through free will. It can never be forced on any of His sacred children.

As said earlier, for timeless eons, God lived in perfect community, love, and companionship with His Holy Spirit and His only begotten Son. Remember that there are three distinct aspects of Almighty God, all three in one and one as three in being. God our Father, the Holy Spirit, and His only begotten son decided to expand their existence by creating sacred children that were made in their Holy image. It was love that drove the expansion of God's being into creating His children with the wonderful gift of free will. This is so God can love them and be loved in return by His children who choose through their free will to love Him in return. This can only increase His great contentment and fulfillment within His boundless eternal existence.

It is extremely important that every child of God knows and understands that it is you and me who are the focus of all creation. Every bit of every creation God has brought into existence was and is for the benefit of His human sacred children. Do not ever forget this.

Our Heavenly Father Loves Us, His Sacred Children, So Much That He Created Two Major Realms of Existence That Have Only One Purpose. To Give All His Children With Their Bi-Dimensional Bodies A Chance to Return to Him in Heavenly Paradise And Live Together for All Eternity.

In order to avoid any confusion This is the list of the three realms that our Heavenly Father has created for us as a mechanism that allows his sacred children to return to the heavenly kingdom.

1. Increasing the size of the spiritual realm to accommodate all his sacred children's needs.
2. The creation of the entire physical realm that we referred to as the universe.
3. Our human bodies that host the real us and serve as a platform to achieve the lifestyle necessary to re-enter the heavenly kingdom

God did create all that you are going to read about for the express benefit of you and me so that we can spend eternity with our loving Father in Heaven if we so choose. It is a terrible shame that so many people today do not understand this and continue to reject our Almighty Father in Heaven. Also, remember that the road to the Heavenly Kingdom is narrow, and the road to Satan's Hell is broad. In another section of this book, I detail the various groups of God's sacred children and their average chances of returning to the Heavenly Kingdom after their time on Earth is finished. Ultimately, whether one person or another makes it back into Heaven always depends on their personal beliefs. Also, on how they lived their life, whether it was according to God's three rules for living your life, which are also in another part of this book.

Note: Only 30% of God's sacred children who come to earth for the earth test make it back into the Heavenly kingdom. This statistic comes directly from our Lord and Savior Jesus Christ. In a later section of this book, you will find many statistics regarding the groups of people on Earth and which ones make it back to the kingdom and which ones do not.

A Few Unique Types of God's Children

The following discussion is not comprehensive, but rather an introduction to some of the ongoing characteristics of life on Earth as we approach the Earth test. When we were all born on this earth, we were all born equal. Yes, I mean that each of us was loved wonderfully, regardless of our physical appearance, race, IQ, or any other characteristic. In fact, in preparation for our life on Earth, we worked with loving angels and other high-ranking individuals in the Kingdom. So that our physical characteristics would assist us in achieving our goals in our upcoming life on Earth. Yes, we do get to choose many life characteristics according to our goals, which are in turn influenced by our physical and spiritual characteristics. And they are much more detailed than the average Christian and or sacred child of God has ever thought possible.

In my personal encounters with people, I have found that there are many characteristics that are individually based. All of God's sacred children are born equal but uniquely different. Each sacred child has a determinative role in shaping the characteristics of their physical body and other spiritual aspects, such as IQ and so on. There are others who follow their own conscience. This is wonderful because it demonstrates a loving connection with Almighty God in our lives.

Our Heavenly Father gave this to all of us before we were born as a moral guide for our lives. Each of us has been given the gift of conscience when we were born. Nobody can ever claim that they did not know God's life rules when they are told because of their earthly behavior, there is no place for them in the Heavenly Kingdom. This is one way of expressing love from our Father in Heaven. But then also, I have encountered people who don't care one way or the other about the existence of God. It seems as if there are endless varieties of sacred children of God, and their life then plays out within the objective reality that exists in the physical realm. These differences in our objective physical reality are what we see every day of our life within the others of God's sacred children.

One very telling signpost of this active rejection of God is spoken phrases they may say, like,

"I will do things my way."

"Do not have time for all that religion stuff. "

"Science says it all, and why do we need to know God to explain things?"

"People who pay no attention to the 10 Commandments and or God's three sacred rules for life on Earth"

There are many more individual situations, all of which lead away from heaven and toward hell.

I have experienced this kind of antagonistic behavior more than once. I pity those people. Because when their day comes, every inkling of their thoughts, attitudes, and emotions against God and Christians alike will be shown to them by Heavenly-loving angels after they pass away. <u>They will be held accountable for all of it</u>, all their destructive attitudes and behaviors. Also, everything good and loving that a child of God does and says is revealed. And it will go very well for their entry back into the Heavenly Kingdom. However, not good for those who spent their lifetime rejecting even the existence of Almighty God, our Heavenly Father.

All of God's children, you and me, are made in His image within the Spiritual and physical realms. But, before God thought our physical universe into existence, He had to prepare many things for us. He brought into existence what we call the physical universe that we know and live in today. Remember, Almighty God exists across the entire timeline that our universe has been created. So, He knows what will happen before it does.

He knew of the coming rebellion of Lucifer. He knew His children would fall into sin, and He decided to save them from sin and redeem them so they could live with Him in paradise for all eternity. But it is up to God's sacred children's free will whether to accept God's offer or not. Remember that our Heavenly Father created us within a blink of an eye. He created each one of us completely unique and different from every other sacred child of His.

All His children stayed within the Heavenly Kingdom for countless eons of time. We played with our loving Father and each other and held for us such delicious, fulfilling, and joyful experiences. During that time with our Father, he educated us in so many aspects of the entirety of The Trinity's existence and how we fit into all of that. We all knew we would have a decision to make. To love God through our free will choice and our Heavenly Father, so we may spend all eternity with Him in the Heavenly Kingdom. Or reject our Almighty Father and choose Satan, succumbing to his temptations, and live a life of evil.

Doing that would result in hell for us and ultimately complete dissolution back into nothingness from which we came. All the above are different types of people, and their variations are brought on by many different factors in people's lives. But the common denominator is their free will choices.

A Wondrous Meeting Place for The Children of God

When you look up at the sky and see billions of stars, you only see a tiny fraction of what God has created for all of us children. It takes not only the stars you can see. But also, astrophysics, astronomy, and other sciences. These sciences tell us that the interaction of billions of galaxies you cannot see is responsible for creating conditions allowing our Earth to remain stable enough for a long enough period to support human life.

We also know that this period is soon coming to an end because of the galactic cycles that prevail. All of this is in the plans of Almighty God. We have great astronomers like Dr. Hugh Ross and many others who do marvelous work that informs us about the timing of the cycles of life. I suggest you read some of his books at books@reason.org. One book is titled "The Improbable Planet." It describes our beloved Earth and all the

Galactic requirements for Earth to exist and support human life. I will give just a few details in the next section.

Our physical universe is a shining example of a highly complex system of interlocking influences, connections, and other codependent processes that provide the necessary conditions for a planet like Earth to exist. Not only to exist but to exist for a long enough time from a biological and physical perspective that supports human life and accomplishes what God wants for his children while they're on earth. These interlocking processes and dependencies across the universe provide a framework that holds the world in the proper position so when God created humans, they could propagate and pass along their heritage to subsequent generations.

One of the astronomical features of our universe is that everything is in a constant state of flux due to countless cycles that come and go in relatively short periods of time. Also, the universe is made up entirely of many distinct kinds of radiation and intense particles at high speeds that would prevent a stable platform for human life to exist. In addition to creation, there is the issue of having a planet be big enough but not too big to accommodate God's for our physical lives. Not only that, but all radiation sources must be far enough away from our solar system so as not to interfere with the physical life form that we call human beings.

Additionally, gravity must be considered. Our bodies can stand the kind of gravity that we have on Earth. Still, throughout the universe, we rarely have an Earth-size planet with just the right amount of oxygen and nitrogen and about 70% water on Earth with a lot of salt. On and on the list goes for the requirements of a planet to support life for only a few tens of thousands of years. It must be long enough for us to live our lives and, in the process, choose if we wish to live with our Heavenly Father or instead reject Him and become a citizen of Hell.

This is so all of God's children can come to earth, discover themselves, and decide through attitudes, emotions, and actions that will determine whether they will spend eternity in the Heavenly Kingdom with their Father. Or will they go to hell and spend eternity with Satan and his demons. This will be before they are dissolved into nothingness using the entropy from which they came—all these physical processes and codependences.

The Creation of the Physical Universe

As hard as it may seem for us, God's sacred children were thought into existence in the blink of an eye. Remember that Almighty God exists in multiple time dimensions simultaneously. The Bible describes one day in Heaven as a thousand years on Earth. We can only imagine what time must translate like in the other dimensions that Almighty God occupies. But from our perspective, our physical universe began approximately 13.8 billion years ago from an extremely hot point of something beyond plasma. It began expanding faster than what we call the speed of light. Astrophysicists refer to this as the period of inflation.

As this book is written, there is late-breaking news that our scientific community of astrophysicists and astronomers have discovered at the very edge of our visible universe. There are quite a few hugely dense formations of glowing matter that do not fall into any of the standard classifications of things like galaxies or nebula and so on.

Nobody knows for sure what they are. It is accurate now to say that astronomers and astrophysicists do not know if our theory, called the Big Bang, adequately explains the origin and growth of our universe. Evidence suggests that we will, at some point, need to revise our Big Bang theory to accommodate the existence of large numbers or groups of material that appear to have predated our Big Bang.

One theory suggests that they may not be from our own universe but rather overlap with another universe. Time will tell if this is true. But the alternatives are fascinating. Scientists today have an enormously comprehensive understanding of our universe, tracing back to when it was only 10^{-43} seconds old. To put this into perspective, this number looks like this:

.0000000000000000000000000000000000000000001 second

It is truly remarkable to consider that we have scientists today who possess an excellent understanding of what God did in the creation of the physical universe. We know what the universe was like immediately after it began to form. Any closer than this 10 X 43rd second before, the math breaks down and becomes indeterminate.

There is an exciting statistic about the first moment of physical creation. Max Planck, a renowned physicist, calculated that the temperature of the tiny sphere from which everything physically originated was 1.416 x 10^32. According to science, that is the maximum possible temperature in any physical structure. You should remember this number because <u>it also means that time began when the universe began.</u> In the book "The Creator and The Cosmos" by Dr. Hugh Ross Ph. D. he wrote, "Of all the Holy books of the religions of the world <u>only the Bible unambiguously states that time is finite</u>. He writes that time has a beginning. That God created time. And that God is capable of cause-and-effect operations before the time dimension of the universe existed, and that God did cause many effects before the time component of our universe existed." [12]

Over time, our physical universe continued to expand in size and cool down from its enormous temperatures. Then atoms and molecules started to form. Then, according to the laws of chemistry molecules, more complex molecules started to form. Then, far more complex minerals began to form. And then, due to the laws of gravity, enormous bodies of matter began to form, and because of these large bodies of matter and their velocity, they started to spin around each other.

Some of these large bodies of matter became so large that they compressed, and their interiors became so hot that they triggered nuclear fusion reactions, releasing enormous amounts of heat. Today, we refer to those globes of extremely hot, spinning matter as stars.

Vast areas of the cosmos became homes to billions and billions of stars, which we now refer to as galaxies. The lifetimes of the stars stretch into

---

[12] The Creator and The Cosmos, Dr, Hugh Ross Ph. D. NavPress. 1993

billions of years. Then, over time, more globular clusters of stars, through gravity, began to spin around themselves, forming spiral galaxies. We refer to the galaxy in which we live as the Milky Way.

The process of forming stars and then galaxies is, one might think, random, but it is not. Early in this process, due to quantum fluctuations, you would find it was far more a clumpy arrangement. Where the globes of stars would attract each other, leaving large holes here and there, or there would be hardly any stars and subsequent galaxies. Over extended periods of time, something extraordinary occurred that our scientists are still puzzled about today: the appearance of what is called dark energy and dark matter. Scientists do not understand what it is. We know it is there, but we cannot measure it directly; we can only measure its effect on the matter that we can see.

At this point, astronomy and astrophysics have been studied using the James Webb Space Telescope. We see that there are galaxies in the outer part of our physical universe that are traveling faster than the speed of light. Yes, they are traveling faster than the speed of light from our perspective within the universe, but it is not that these galaxies are breaking the physical laws regarding the speed of light. They are, in fact, inhabiting a part of the physical universe that is expanding greater than the speed of light. These galaxies are along for the ride. It is the very space of the universe that is expanding faster and faster, not the individual galaxies.

As time goes on, we will see fewer and fewer of these galaxies as they disappear into the distance. Also, we are seeing fewer and fewer stars as they disappear into the distance as well. If this continues in our universe, the visible universe we see will become to the point where it will be only the Earth that we see. And then, finally, our Earth will dissolve as well into nothingness. For those who believe in our Father Almighty, we will be in a timeless eternity with infinite fulfillment with our Father in Heaven. And the physicality of the universe will in no way affect us at all. But remember, dear sacred child; there will come a time in which the physical universe will no longer exist because at that time, whenever it occurs, our Heavenly Father will have completed our Heavenly existence. There will no longer be any need for His sacred children to come to Earth and take the Earth Test.

Everything I talked about led to our night sky, blessed with ever so many beautiful star formations and the Milky Way. Away from light pollution and smog, in very dark areas, you can see the Milky Way as a band of dense stars that stretches across the sky from one side to the other. I saw this when I was on a cruise ship in the middle of the Atlantic Ocean. The captain was kind enough to shut off the upper deck lights, so it was perfect conditions to see God's magnificent creation with my own eyes and the group of people I was with. And to think that some people in science believe all of it was a random event resulting from a quantum fluctuation.

That is just plain BS. Being a scientist does not prove you are correct. The truth of everything is available to the children of God who believe in the Lord Jesus Christ and our Almighty Father in Heaven along with their Holy Spirit, which proceeds from them.

Remember these key points:

1. I have discussed the creation of the physical realm that we refer to as the universe. It had a finite starting point within the dimension of time. The collective understanding is that the universe began 13.7 billion years ago based on our timeline.

2. This physical realm allows our physical bodies to host our Personal Heavenly Spirits within them, which in turn allows God's children to directly interact with the Spiritual realm.

3. This interaction occurs within our minds / Spiritual bodies. It is our minds that determine the actions we take in the physical realm. That is acted out with our physical bodies. It is through our bodily actions in the physical realm that we broadcast to the world and the Spiritual realm what is inside our minds and Spirits.

4. What we do within the physical world directly affects our minds and spirit, as well as the lives of others of God's children around us.

5. The results of our actions provide us with feedback on our value system and other characteristics that are contained within our minds and, most importantly, within our Spirits.

6. The wise person will use this physical realm feedback to change what is contained within their mind and Spiritual being. In this way, we can consciously move closer to Almighty God and His divine will for us.

7. Most people make the mistake of thinking that, "I am here, and God is somewhere over there." That is entirely wrong. When our Heavenly Father created each of us as unique, sacred children of His, he loved us so much that he left a part of Himself within our Spiritual being. Additionally, there is nowhere in creation where God is not. All of creation is contained within our loving Almighty Father. Remember what the psalmist said, "no matter where I go, You are there."

8. Without the physical realm, we would not be able to change and would not be able to overcome our sinful nature handed down to us by Adam and Eve, called Original Sin by Christians.

9. It is only within the physical realm that allows us to change ourselves and, therefore, our Spiritual being. God can meet us one-on-one within our Spiritual minds while we remain in the physical realm for a time. It is here that we can confess our sins to our Almighty Father and ask for His forgiveness and guidance in all that we say and do for the rest of our lives. If we are sincere in our Spiritual hearts when asking for forgiveness and guidance, then I believe our Father will certainly forgive us of our sins. In doing so, you have become a new creation.

10. Both the Spiritual realm and the physical realm have been carefully crafted by our Almighty Father to connect with our

physical bodies and our Spiritual minds. Without this creation, we would have no opportunity to choose our Father and spend all eternity with Him in a perfect paradise that surpasses our imagination, even while on earth.

11. The physical part of our existence and our physical bodies are designed so as to propagate God's children throughout many generations across time. This is necessary because there are far more of God's Spiritual children waiting in the Heavenly realm than would fit on this planet all at once. They wait for their opportunity to come to earth and live their life to choose with our free will our Almighty Father over Satan and live in paradise with Him.

12. Before God's only begotten son, our Lord and Savior Jesus Christ, came to earth, there was no connection between God's children on earth and our Heavenly Father. It was Jesus Christ who restored this Holy connection so that once we chose our Heavenly Father, we would ascend back from where we came, which is from the Heavenly Kingdom. Rejecting our Lord Jesus Christ dooms that person to a significantly shortened existence as entropy ultimately dissolves them back into nothingness from where they came. It must be this way, for the alternative is to allow sin back into the Holy Kingdom. That cannot and will not ever happen.

Now, let us proceed to a detailed examination of what it took for God to create the physical realm we call the universe. It is far more complex than what we can imagine because of all the intricate systems within the universe of irreducible complexity. The mechanisms within our universe have many tightly bound parameters that, if not there, the universe would not be able to support a singular planet called Earth. Nor be able to support human life, which is the will of God.

Everything is in motion, including our beloved Earth. At some time in the future, the Earth will be exposed to far more radiation and forces of gravity from other stars, especially the Andromeda Galaxy, as we get closer and closer. This will make life on Earth increasingly impossible. Earth was chosen because its location is in the Milky Way Galaxy, and the Milky Way Galaxy is in an area that is stable. For now, the Earth is stable long enough for the miracle of life to be hosted on Earth in all its splendor and stay stable long enough to accommodate our human physical needs.

11

Time and Dimensions

Everything is So Flexible

Within the realm where time and dimension are flexible at the wishes of Almighty God, nothing is fixed like concrete as it appears to all of us for now. Throughout our entire lives, we encounter the spatial dimensions and the dimension of time as being reliably fixed and not changing. However, just as a reference, remember that it is within the Heavenly power of Almighty God to change the dimensions and include time to do so for a purpose they have in mind. In this book, I have multiple times referred to time as flexible when I said things like, "in the blink of an eye," etc. It is true for what I described.

This also applies to special dimensions. Nobody knows how big our Heavenly Father is. As an example, our known universe is approximately 92 trillion light years in diameter. It is expanding at a rate that is faster than the speed of light. The astronomical phenomena we saw last night can no longer be seen this week or next. They traveled outside of our visible universe limits due to the fast increase in the diameter of our universe.

We know that our Heavenly Father is within our universe, but he is also outside of it into a spatial area that we don't know anything about, but he created that also.

The Size of God and The Created Realms

It is only the highly educated and wise that would even venture into speculating upon how big our Heavenly Father is. You really cannot put dimensions on Him or the Holy Spirit or our Lord and Savior, Jesus

Christ. Each of his sacred children, meaning you and me, have limitations about our physical size, both spiritually and physically.

Regarding our loving Heavenly Father, the best we can do is to realize that he is in, around, and through all creation. God's presence includes smaller than the smallest spatial dimension that science has discovered, which is far smaller than quarks that make up neutrons, protons and the electrons that comprise all the physical matter on Earth. God's presence also includes endless dimensions beyond the size of our universe.

It has been said regarding the size of God was that He could be thought of as a circle. His center would be infinite in size in all directions, not just two dimensions but at least four or more dimensions. Additionally, our Heavenly Father's circumference of that gets complex and has the circumstance to the X power. His circumference would have no end.

The best way to think of how large is God is to point in a random direction and realize that the line that you are creating has no end in any direction. Now, the opposite is also true. Think about going inward. First, you will encounter cellular structures. Then you will discover individual cells that are all linked together to perform a particular function. inside of that there is a single structure of protoplasm that is contained within a single cell. The amount of complexity within one singular cell is enormous. Biological activity within a cell is more complex than at the nuclear level of atoms.

Digging deeper, we get to the molecular level which is individual clumps of atoms coming together to form a molecule that has specific properties. Digging deeper yet into the individual atoms, you will run into the strong nuclear force and the weak nuclear force that binds the protons and neutrons together. Digging deeper still taking protons and neutrons as examples are made up of quarks which can be up quarks down quarks and a few others as well like a quark called charm.

The reason I tell you all this is to make this singular point.

Our Holy Trinity when they created our physical universe did indeed create everything from the simplest quark of an atom all the way up

to the largest astrophysical galaxies we find within the universe. And our Heavenly Father can be found in all of it. This includes the other two members of The Trinity, Jesus Christ, and the Holy Spirit themselves. I repeat, our Heavenly Father can be found from the smallest particle up through the largest interstellar formation.

The psalmist said, "No matter where I go, you are there." Psalm 139:7–12:

But the story does not end with the above scientific explanations of things. When each of us were created in the blink of an eye,

Our Heavenly Father loved us so very much He left a part of Himself within our Spiritual hearts, which will always be with us, no matter where we go, what we do, or anything else.

All three members of The Trinity were lovingly placed within our hearts before we were born on this earth.

It can, therefore, be accurately said that our Heavenly Father and the other two members of The Trinity are found within each and every one of us. This fact is also the basis by which every one of us can be accurately and lovingly judged regarding our life on earth and how we live our lives. It is because Almighty God knows everything that is ever said and everything that is ever thought, and all the emotions and motivations can be accurately known by The Trinity. It is in this way that a complete and accurate judgment of every sacred child on earth can be derived from. Remember, I have said earlier there are no secrets.

What I just told you is an enormous and loving piece of understanding who our Heavenly Father is. At our birth that individual piece of Almighty God had already been embedded within our hearts. It serves as a beacon of love and truth connected to our Heavenly Father, Jesus Christ, and the Holy Spirit. Little children already have a sense of what is right and what is wrong. It is foundational to think that little children already have an accurate understanding of how to behave in this physical life we call Earth. Little children already know the foundational elements of right and wrong after they are born on this earth.

If a sacred child of God dies and claims to our Heavenly Savior he did not know of God's rules, which he says explain all his sins, that is entirely false. It cannot be used as any kind of explanation for all his sins against others of God's sacred children. <u>There are no excuses.</u>

So, in summary, regarding the size of our Heavenly Triad, there is no accurate measurement that can be made because everything is in a state of flux and is growing faster and faster. This even applies to the microscopic and atomic levels, but nobody discusses that aspect of things. If an atom of hydrogen grows by some amount, we would never really know it because everything around it would grow proportionately then our measurements would remain the same.

The bottom line is that not only is the universe growing at a faster rate, but, importantly, our Heavenly Father is with us all the time. He is within our very being, our very physical and Spiritual bodies. He is within each of us and our thought processes and everything that we say that we do, that we touch. I find this incredibly comforting to know that our Heavenly Father loves each of us so very much that he left a part of Himself within us. That is a great comfort for me, and I believe it is also great comfort for you once you think about it.

Even from the perspective of prayer, this means it is utterly impossible for anyone to say a prayer and for God not to hear it. For he is right there with you every moment of every day, and it is impossible for our Heavenly Father not to listen to what you have to say. And be open to what His responses to your prayers may be.

These facts of our life fit ever so well with what the Apostle John said in Chapter 3, Verse 16. "For God so loved the world that He gave His only begotten Son, that whoever believes in Him should not perish but have everlasting life."

Jesus Christ
October 4, 2024

My dearest of dear sons, thank you for asking me this question about time and dimensions and how they can be flexible if we wish. All of that

which you said is completely true. Our sacred children do not have the power to change any of the dimensions but those of us within The Trinity do have that. For your lives, we decided on several different capabilities or powers that we felt you needed to be successful in the physical realm. I believe each of you has done a very good job of using those powers constructively for the benefit of all others of your Heavenly Father's sacred children. However, in recent history, there has been an increasing number of your Father's sacred children who have been abusing their powers. They do this to gain for more terrestrial power over others of God's children and to enrich themselves with money that will disappear on the day of their deaths.

As you have pointed out, my dear son, so accurately, the End of Times began in the 1960s on earth and is now beginning to unfold as prophesied in <u>biblical literature</u>. Although this may be off the point, I feel an urgent need to repeat what I have said in your other writings about the End of Times. <u>The people in Europe will experience the full terror and suffering of the End of Times. Mostly because they let into their countries the Satanic minions of Satan called Muslims that will wreak havoc and suffering among ever so many millions that live in Europe.</u> My dear son, as you have stated before, <u>Islam is indeed the religion of Satan</u>. As this is written,

<u>I want to emphasize again that Donald Trump will be your next president. And he will have a monstrously large task ahead of Him to undo all the Satanic damage that was purposely caused by your Joe Biden administration.</u> [13]

Note: Please pay particular attention to what our Lord and Savior Jesus says in this following paragraph. See how he and I are ever so close together that he can instantly discern what my emotional state is. This is just not for me, my dear sacred reader. Jesus has the full ability to do this for every one of God's sacred children. Our Blessed Mother Mary, when

---

[13] This comment from Jesus Christ was written many months before the Election in November 2024

I was writing with her, there were several occasions when discussing the End of Times, she perceived how upset I was about the awful suffering that is coming to Earth.

My dearest son, I can tell right now that you're getting depressed again by what I have just said to you. Lift your heart, my dear son you know how close I am to you always and I always will be along with your Blessed Mother Mary. At this time, I know you're wondering if you should leave the San Jose area and I told you to hold off on that for a while which you have done. However, it is getting nearer to the point in California where crime is increasing and is increasingly out of control. So, I suggest, my dear son, that you start looking for a place to live that is near your family in the places we have spoken about earlier.

As I also said earlier, your country will not bear the brunt of the End of Times but rather it will still feel the damages done by the Democrat party in your country. I want so very much for your entire family to not experience what the End of Times is bringing to the world and to a lesser degree your country, America. You and your family are very well protected as you know but there are some things you must do also which I know you will.

I love you so very much, my dearest son, your Lord and Savior Jesus

12

What Is Life? Where Did It Come From?

Spiritual Life and Spiritual Bodies

Now, because of my extensive Spiritual life, while I have been on planet Earth, I do know a few people personally that are currently in hell. I know them personally. One of them chose to be there because she was given two chances to reconcile her behavior with the requirements for all people who live in our eternal paradise. To her, Heaven brought with it just too many behavioral requirements. So, she decided she did not want to adhere to that, and so this woman decided to go back into hell. Originally, I thought no one would ever do that. But I was wrong.

I knew her for a time before she died, and she appeared to be screaming and screeching because demons were clawing at her like you could not possibly believe. I guided her to our Lord and Savior Jesus Christ, telling her that he would take her to heaven. I have covered this in more detail in another part of this book. So, I'll just say that she went to heaven, and like many people, they could not stand the rules of life due to her violent upbringing while taking the Earth test.

Her upbringing as a child was almost identical to mine, Except the cruelty and the violence came from her mother, not like me from my father.

It was at my request that our Lord and Savior Jesus Christ brought her back out of Hell to give her a second chance to live in the paradise of the Heavenly Kingdom. Sadly, she wanted to do things her way and not God's way; therefore, she chose hell again and was escorted back through the gates of Hell. She will ultimately dissolve back into nothingness. Nothingness, by the way, also means that there will not be any memories of those people who are in hell because their memory is something, and nothingness means just that. Nothingness means that there can be no memories of these people who reside within our minds to a certain point.

It is our Spiritual bodies that give life to our physical bodies. It is our Heavenly Father, along with His only begotten son and the Holy Spirit, which precedes from them, that give life to every one of us. It is our Spiritual bodies that are the real us of who and what we really are! It is our eternal spiritual selves that live on for all eternity within the Heavenly Kingdom, which is a paradise created just for all our Heavenly Father's sacred children.

Remember as stated earlier in this book, all of us were created by our Heavenly Father unknown billions of years ago. Every one of us was and remains a Spiritual being made in the image of our Heavenly Father. While we were within the Heavenly Kingdom, we were educated to a great degree by Heavenly angels and other loving Spiritual beings.

What Is Life?

All of us already know about our physical bodies. Democrats say that life does not go any farther than that. That is certainly what Satan wants us all to believe because it cuts our loving Heavenly Father out of the picture.

However, every one of God's sacred children are spiritual in nature and are eternal in their lives. So, what is life?

Life is…

What is the ultimate origin of our life?

We know that we are not a pile of accidental chemicals that, over time, bumping into each other somehow formed our physical bodies. That is complete and utter nonsense. There is no secular explanation of where our bodies come from, and certainly NOT where our spiritual bodies come from either. Does anyone think that Charles Darwin had the Magic Formula many decades ago for where our bodies come from? If anybody believes that they are sadly mistaken. I bet many of them do not realize if they believe that hogwash Darwinian interpretation by putting words in Charles's mouth, they also are automatically denying the existence of

Almighty God. And they are denying the very source of their own existence.

It is incredible that some people are so ignorant and gullible. They believe a botanist who worked for a few months in the Galapagos Islands produced a theory that explains all human life is just beyond anything that has the slightest tendency of intelligence to it. Now, I am not a Darwin hater by any means. In fact, I consider Him to be a very good scientist and botanist. In his book The Origin of the Species, he said if shown the changes in a species over time cannot be explained by a sequence of many minor changes, then my theory is wrong. I recommend his book to anybody, frankly.

Human beings have two magnificent parts to them. One is, of course, our physical body. The second one is far more important, and that is our spiritual body. Our physical body can only last from 70 to 90 years before major portions of it stop working and it dies. However, our spiritual body keeps on existing for all eternity. Other sections in this book explain this in detail.

All life originates from Our Heavenly Almighty Father. Yes! All life, no matter what form it takes. When it comes to our Heavenly Father, He loved us so much when he loved us into existence that He left inside of our spiritual selves part of his own consciousness, part of Himself. It's accurate saying our Heavenly Father, Lord Jesus Christ, and the Holy Spirit do indeed love us so very much that they participate without us knowing it. They participate in our lives, our love, our struggles, our worries and everything else. We're inseparable from them, and they are inseparable from us.

I will give you one example. When I was writing the book titled **God's Grand Design, Blessed Mother Mary Speaks, Her Apparitions, The End of Times**. Mother Mary was with me constantly, and as I was writing this book, she was ever so close to me. And when I came up with some descriptions of things, Blessed Mother Mary was right there suggesting how to phrase things and the content of them.

The title of that book that Mother Mary and I co-wrote together is **God's Grand Design, Blessed Mother Mary Speaks of Her Apparitions and The End of Times**. Now, frequently, because of documenting the horrific events coming our way during the End of Times, I would get quite upset just visualizing the awful suffering that will happen to people living on Earth. I never said anything, but Blessed Mother Mary knew I was getting very upset, and she offered to, on several occasions, stop the writing process for a while so I could recover my emotions. Yes, my dear sacred child of God, we are indeed that close to each other. She is in Heaven, and I am on Earth.

Yet, I will tell you something else about my personal existence. For the last number of years both our Lord and Savior Jesus Christ and our Blessed Mother Mary have been no more than 12 inches away from my left shoulder and my right shoulder. We can speak to each other any time we wish about anything we want. This is because I am our Almighty Fathers Anointed Messenger. This is all I want to say for now.

13

The Loving Divine Unity of All Life and Existence Ultimate Origin

Everything within creation exists from and is part of Almighty God. Another way to look at this is quite simple. If it exists, the ultimate source of its existence is from our Heavenly Father, our Almighty Father. It is our Heavenly Father who is the source of all that is within the physical realm and all that is within the Spiritual realm. There are no exceptions whatsoever. Additionally, this is not a case where God created everything and then removed Himself to observe and see what happens.

The opposite is true. Our Heavenly Father is within every particle of existence, whether it be Spiritual or physical. This is especially true regarding His sacred beloved children who are created in His image. This is both you and me. We are very special creations for several reasons.

1. We are the only ones that are made in the image of our Heavenly Father.

2. We are temporary physical beings. However, due to the physical forces scientists call entropy and what Jesus Christ calls the law of disintegration, our physical bodies will last for only a relatively brief time. Then they stop functioning, and our Spiritual selves continue onward in their eternal life. When you wake up in the morning and look in the mirror, you might see a new itty-bitty wrinkle on your face or a new gray hair that you have not noticed before. It is these kinds of things that emerge over time, providing direct evidence of entropy or the law of disintegration.

Have you ever noticed that regardless of how many years have passed by you still feel like yourself, not physically but from your self-identity which gains wisdom and knowledge along the way?

3. We are permanently Spiritual beings also made within the image of our Heavenly Father. It is our Spiritual beings that live onward for all eternity. This is with one exception. That exception is only if a sacred child of God rejects our loving Heavenly Father. And they live their life in a way that proves beyond a doubt that they do reject our Heavenly Father's rules of existence and life. The way a sacred child lives their life is proof positive testimony that reveals whether they love our Heavenly Father or not. All the evidence resides within the tapestry of our lives.

Elsewhere within this book, I have made significant efforts to show the different categories of people on the earth. I've split them up many ways so you can get an excellent idea of the chances of various kinds of people going to Heaven or not.

4. Because we are both Spiritual and physical beings, the Spiritual part of us is highly connected with the Heavenly realm. This means our Heavenly Father, our Lord and Savior Jesus Christ, the Holy Spirit, which proceeds outward from them, and even our Blessed Mother Mary.

5. The Spiritual part of us is enormously wonderful. Why? It is because when each of us were created in the blink of an eye, our Heavenly Father loved us each so very much that he left part of Himself within us. This means that it is never a case of you being here and God being way over there somewhere else. Our Heavenly Father is not only within every particle of what he created but he is also within every one of our Spiritual bodies.

It is impossible for our Heavenly Father not to hear every one of our prayers. It is also impossible for our Heavenly Father not to be totally aware of everything that we say, everything that we do, everything that we think, everything that we feel, and so on. It is in this way The Trinity knows completely every tiny aspect of our entire lives and everything we experience and everything that we feel. It is in this way that it is impossible for Almighty God not to hear every one of our prayers no matter how insignificant it may seem to us.

This is also true when it comes to the moments after our physical bodies pass away. Our Heavenly Father is loving, he is just, and fair. It is in this way that each of our destinations, Heaven or hell, will be determined from an absolutely pure and perfect perspective.

Most people on the street when you ask them whether they believe in God or not most will tell you they're not sure. If they say they believe in God, then they really do not understand much of anything about who God is and how he plays a vital role in their lives.

Usually, people think of God in terms of spatial distance between themselves and God living somewhere else up high in Heaven somehow. People believe that God is up high somewhere, and Satan is under the ground somewhere and we human beings are somehow stuck in the middle on the surface of the Earth. But that's about it. Fundamentally people are exceedingly ignorant about the one true God that Christians know quite a bit about. Yet even with Christians they do not fully understand just how Almighty God is within us and around us. This is because most Christians do not give the Holy Trinity much thought.

The best way to understand different facets of existence both Spiritual and physical think of the Spiritual realm and in the physical realm as being intertwined together with our Almighty Father at its very center.

Almighty God is everywhere both in terms of the Spiritual realm and the physical realm. St Peter said in one of the psalms that no matter where he went our Heavenly Father was already there.

So, the very quick answer, to the question, "What Is Life" You simply answer by saying all life proceeds from our Heavenly Father and goes outward from Him and in its various forms. From this moment on I know our Lord and savior Jesus Christ has several things he wants to emphasize to all of you, and I want our Lord to add to anything I just said.

14

A Poetic View of God's Creations

Author's Comments:

Both creation and redemption are intimately linked. The Reason for creation is to allow redemption for God's sacred Children. The spiritual realm, the physical realm, and the finely tuned characteristics of our physical body are all designed for one purpose. That is so we, God's sacred children, can occupy these creations in a manner that allows us to use the magnificent power of our free will to choose which manner of life we wish to live. Is it to live our life of love, peace, sincerity, of acceptance of our Heavenly Father's Ways of life? Or do we choose to reject our Heavenly Father? It really is just that simple.

What Is Redemption?

Redemption simply means that through the way we live on earth, we demonstrate to the Holy Trinity we choose the way of life of our Almighty Father and totally reject the horrific sin of Satan. For most of our Father's sacred children, sadly, they end up rejecting the life rules and commandments of our Heavenly Father and subsequently condemn themselves to hell.

I must point out that our Heavenly Father **never condemns anyone to hell**. That is just not in His nature or character. Many people think so. But it is false. It is the sinners that will condemn themselves to hell and ultimately complete disintegration back to the nothingness from which they have been created from. During everyone's life review after death in the most loving environment imaginable, everything you have ever said, done, thought, and felt during your life on earth is reviewed with infinite detail. It becomes extremely clear through this review whether you have lived your life in accordance with God's rules of life or not.

It will then become terribly obvious to everyone which destination is in their future based on how they lived their lives. Is it the Heavenly Kingdom, or is it hell? It is the child of God who will clearly know that it is heaven if they are qualified for it. If their life has been wretch, there is only one path forward for them, and that is to go to hell. And this is what they will condemn themselves to do.

Both are finely tuned to the tight specifications of the human body, both physical and biological. Additionally, The Trinity's astrological creation is finely tuned to the hyper-tight specifications of the earth to support human life for long periods of time. Also, the cosmos is finely tuned to support the Milky Way galaxy to support our earth for long periods of time to support human life for long periods of time. Break one link in that chain, and no human life will ever be possible!

Our story begins…

A Poem of God's Sacred Love

God is the essence of all that is true, all that is good, all that is love.

Fly into our hearts, dear Lord, like a white and pure beautiful dove.

The Trinity all together, one yet three, three yet one,

To save us from sin, he sent us His son.

Total fulfillment, a time before time, the bedrock of the universe, the foundation of all, is one

God's cornerstone of all that is truth exists complete with deep adoration.

Lacking nothing, they increased their joy, created us children, to God we cleave.

Made in His image and ever so pure. We came to life, Adam and Eve

God certainly lives from the stars through space; remember, He loves you and me.

Coming together, His divine nurturing is what we desperately need.

But if without it, we will wither away, yes indeed!

The words of God to us nurturing so infinite and precise,

Look at the Mandelbrot; only perfection could ever suffice.

Father knew His sacred children salvation they needed even before Adam's fall.

So, we will prepare creation, not one but three unseen realms also to be.

The first creation was indeed very special, built for sinners just like you, just like me.

The first for my children is a physical body choice to grow and love close to Me.

Second, the physical realm, to decide whether it is Satan or is it Me

Free will to choose our Almighty Father, if so, forgiven now for all eternity.

The third with Spiritual life for children forgiven, live within Me, The Trinity all three.

To create a universe for all to pass His test, love, and accept His infinite glory.

Given a choice in this second creation, to God the forgiven, we will certainly go.

On Earth, a planet fine-tuned for us, a path to our Father and spiritually grow.

These are the creations meant only for us, a path to God and our eternal home.

15

The Heavenly Realm

The Heavenly Kingdom: A Description [14]

I consider myself to be a normal Christian. Our Heavenly Father refers to me as His <u>special sacred child who is also His anointed messenger</u>. And this is accepted. And being a Christian, I have had many questions about the nature and characteristics of what Heaven is really like. We all have heard many stories about this and the other thing regarding Heaven. It is also described in the Bible. But I wanted to use my remarkably close loving relationship with Almighty God to explore deeper into the truth of what Heaven is. This is not comprehensive by any means, but it does shed a lot of light on our understanding of the Heavenly realm. It is a given that Heaven is a Spiritual place and not a physical one.

First, here are a few representations from Biblical literature that describe our Heavenly destiny.

In the books of Genesis, Exodus, Leviticus, Deuteronomy, and all the other Old Testament books, Heaven is described as "all that is above earth and where the stars are." An extremely basic and fundamental understanding.

In the New Testament, starting with the book Matthew. Heaven now has a different identity. Matthew refers to Heaven as "the Kingdom of Heaven." It also becomes the place where our Father, Almighty God, comes from. It is the home of God within the Kingdom of Heaven. It is also the dwelling place for the Son of Man, meaning the Lord Jesus Christ and the Angels, as described in the Gospel of Mark.

---

[14] God's Grand Design of All Creation for Your Redemption

It was also the home for Lucifer, the angel until he rebelled against God and fell like lightning from Heaven in the book of Luke. Heaven is also characterized as a sanctuary. In the book of Revelation. Heaven is also characterized as the source of Godly power, grace, and everlasting joy for those who accept Almighty God's love.

Some Detailed Questions About the Heavenly Kingdom

With all of this in mind, I have a few questions that I would love to have our Heavenly Father give us further knowledge about.

My questions were:

1. Has the Heavenly realm been in existence for eternity like the Holy Trinity?

2. What are some details of the Heavenly realm? Describe the realm of Almighty God.

3. What is its size relative to the Spiritual realm and the physical realm?

4. How are its borders protected from evil, from Satan and his demons?

5. Is there truly only one entrance or gate that allows entry into the Heavenly realm?

I sat down with my laptop and meditated with these questions in my mind about Heaven. I prayed to our Lord in Heaven and asked if he would respond, knowing that I would publish this in my seventh book. Graciously, with such warmth and love, God answered my prayer, and His revelation and words are below. You are holding the only book in Christian literature that has permission from Almighty God, and the author is allowed to print that for the benefit of all His sacred children.

With all this in mind, we have come to a particularly important and interesting section of this book. That is, with the help of Almighty God, it is to describe what Heaven is like. We know it is far different than this Satan-drenched earth we live in now. As time goes on, circumstances on earth are only getting worse and worse. So, let us concentrate on what our Christian future is.

July 30, 2022
5:28 PM

Our Lord and Savior Jesus Christ Answers the Questions Above

"My dear children, The Trinity has always lived in the Heavenly realm. It has no beginning; it exists now and will live on. It is eternal, whereas what you call time in the physical realm does not exist. Heaven is all around you, whether you realize it or not. Heaven is also a place. <u>*Within this realm, different forms of life exist within The Trinity: Almighty God our Father, me, who is His only begotten son, and the Holy Spirit, which precedes from us within The Trinity outward to the other realms of existence.*</u> [15]

And that includes, of course, our sacred children made in our image. Size-wise, which is something our children can relate to, Heaven has no outer boundaries, and within it, it contains all the other Spiritual realms that you have described within this magnificent book. As you know, my son, we within The Trinity are pure Spiritual beings encompassing the entire realm of Heaven. Again, it is infinite in all the multiple dimensions that your scientists are working on, and it contains all the different time dimensions as well.

It is exceedingly easy for us within The Trinity to use all these different dimensions of space, time, and other aspects of dimensionality. To serve us in The Trinity to explore an infinite different variety of attributes,

---

[15] One of the most magnificent and loving aspects of all our existence is the following. Absolutely everything, including all realms of existence, all of God's sacred children, and all of the physical and spiritual realms, exist within our Father Almighty. To keep things very simple, earlier or somewhere else in this book of our Father's love, I presented the fact that our Heavenly father has loved us so very much That he left part of Himself Within us, within our spiritual being. However, that was a truthful thing to say about our Heavenly father, but it did not go far enough. The rest of the existential truth of our glorious Heavenly father is simply that absolutely everything within existence is also contained within our loving, almighty father.

qualities, and intense love from each of us in The Trinity back to the others.

Within your book, dear son, you are exploring the characteristics and nature of the physical realm, the Spiritual realm, and now the Heavenly realm. There are other realms, but none of those pertain to your existence within our divine goals for you, our children. We within The Trinity are easily able to create more dimensions and more realms of existence if we so choose, and that serves our purpose.

Remember, all that is needed is a thought to bring something into existence, and it is done. What you call Heaven has been our home from before eternity began. I know to you that sounds like an oxymoron, but it is not. Considering all the different dimensions that you are unaware of, that statement is not understandable.

Yet, it is true. You asked for a more detailed definition of what the Heavenly realm is like. It is not like the physical realm or the Spiritual realm that you currently reside in. Its laws of physics, for example, are very different than those on Earth within the physical realm. There is far more freedom to come and go as you wish without any effort on your part. All you need to do is think about where you want to be, and you may want it for you to be there. All communications within our sacred children, the Angels, and, of course, us within The Trinity are as you would call telepathic. That is not to say that there is no sound in the Heavenly realm; it is quite the opposite. Your Lord Father in Heaven loves to hear the angels sing, and he loves to hear the voices of His children such as yourself. If you cannot sing on earth, that is certainly not a problem, for you will be surprised at how deliciously wonderful you will sound in the Heavenly realm.

Angels will come and go and be with you as your constant companion if you wish. All of you will know each other and their stories of each other and their struggles on earth if that is what you wish. The depth of love that you will feel within the Heavenly realm is far more intense and pleasurable than you can imagine.

My son, I know you remember the golden orb that appeared to you on the jet halfway across the Pacific Ocean. That is when you were told the following words, "God loves you." Along with that simple message came a magnificently intense feeling of love for you. I know you felt like running up and down the aisle of the jet proclaiming that God loves us. It is good that you did not choose to, for that would have created such an incident of confusion among the other people that it would not be good for them.

As I said earlier, the realms of existence are contained within Heavenly. But this does not mean in any way things cannot flow into and out of the Heavenly realm without strong conditions and protection from Satan and his demons. The Heavenly realm, with all its different physics and roles of Spirituality, is completely fortified from any intrusion from those Spirits that do not belong there, no matter how small the intrusion might be.

Within the Heavenly realm, there are different layers of existence. There are seven layers, to be exact. And each of the ascending layers becomes filled with more and more gratification, fulfillment, intensifying love, and other rewards. Rewards consistent with what each of our children has shown themselves to be while they are on the earth.

Remember, my son, that the creation of the physical and Spiritual realms is matched perfectly with the design of your human body. This is so the needs of your physical body are met with the resources available to you on earth. And as I said before, it is your brain and the overlying Spiritual body that you have that is entirely in tune with the Spiritual realm.

Many people have speculated on the size of the Holy Kingdom where God Almighty resides and where the Holy Spirit and I call home. All our creations are from our Heavenly realm. Your Father so loves His children not only after you were thought into existence, all being individually different from every other, you lived with your Father in Heaven as Spiritual beings for a long time. This is so he can enjoy each of you personally. And love you in the ways that match your talents, your attributes, your characteristics and what has been decided will be the trajectory of your life once you are born on earth.

What your Biblical literature says about the details of which God knows each of you when it says Almighty God even knows the number of hairs on your head is so true. For Almighty God resides not only in and through all of creation, but we also know every detail of your life. We know your motivations, and everything you say and do, for it is in this way that we can separate the sheep from the goats. There are no secrets within all of creation.

The size of the Heavenly Kingdom is, on purpose, smaller than what I described Heaven to be, for the Heavenly Kingdom where we in The Trinity reside necessarily is smaller. Yet for our children that join us within the Heavenly realm eternally, it will seem unending in every way. There will be no restrictions upon the children of God. Yet, at the same time, there will be some responsibilities for each of our sacred children. However, this is a very light load, for the Heavenly realm is meant to be a paradise for all our Father's children.

Our children will have all of creation at their feet to explore and wonder what their Heavenly Father created for them. Remember all of creation that you see in the Heavens above. And this bears within you and other things are specifically designed to create a pathway from the wreckage in your minds that has been caused by Lucifer, now known as Satan, and all his demons.

As some of your poets have said, if there is a key to the gates of Heaven, it can be stated as belief and faith in me as your Lord and Savior. Also love in your hearts for all your fellow children of God.

You asked how the Kingdom of God in Heaven is protected from those who do not belong. There are several ways that this is accomplished, but you will not understand them. But one way that you will is the many mighty angels that we have that can keep things well in order based on the will of your Father.

Is there one gate to the entrance of Heaven? Yes, my son, there is only one path to the Heavenly realm and one gate. Only those found in the Book of Life and that have kept the word of your Father in Heaven love others of His children as you love yourself and the commandments God gave to Moses.

Entrance is only those that find their names in the sacred book. And as you and I have discussed before, only a few will find their names written

in this book of life. There are many more things I could tell you, my dear son, but I believe this will answer your questions and the understanding of the nature of existence by all your readers. Those who decide to take the time and effort to read the words contained in this magnificent book you have written with of course the help we give you from The Trinity.

I love you, my dear son."

More Questions for Almighty God

After several weeks from the revelation that God has provided for His children who read this book, I developed some more questions. I wanted to ask Almighty God our Father about the Heavenly realm and God's sacred children who now live there. They are as follows,

1. Can you please describe whether a sacred child can advance to higher levels within the Heavenly realm after they are already there? I know our Father continually encourages additional growth, understanding, and learning. So, there must be opportunities for us as children to do this while in Heaven.

2. Am I correct? the above answers to my initial questions, you stated that **"Within this realm** (the Heavenly)**, there are different forms of life that exist."** You mentioned some of them we already know about. However, are there others? It would not be surprising that since The Trinity is infinite, there would be many other forms of life.

3. Dear Lord, you mentioned the following, which surprised me. **"Heaven has no outer boundaries; within it, it contains all the other Spiritual realms."** I never thought of Heaven as containing all the other realms. Does this mean that the Heavenly realm overlaps in some manner all other realms? Is Heaven integrated with the different realms? Or are they in some fashion side-by-side except for the Spiritual realm overlapping with the physical realm so God's sacred children can employ both their Spiritual minds and their physical bodies?

4. Does this mean also that the Heavenly realm contains the realm that we call hell? In the gospel of Luke, he describes Lucifer as being cast down and out of Heaven, and he became Satan, the prince of the earth. This terminology of up-and-down indicates that there may be some dimensionality within the Heavenly realm. Is this correct?

5. On a different note, because this question just occurred to me, my dear Almighty God, creator of all things seen and unseen, what is your definition of "life." I have my definition, but my definition does not count. It is your definition and description that is of

supreme importance. I would love to know, and all your sacred children also want to know about this answer.

6. ***"There are no secrets within all of creation." You mentioned this in the text above.*** This comes as no surprise. However, would you, dear Lord, go into more detail regarding the impossibility of secrets within creation? Also, what are the reasons that creation is this way?

7. ***"Yet eternally for our children that join us within the Heavenly realm, it will seem unending in every way. There will be no restrictions upon the children of God." I have a practical example and a question for you.*** As a pilot with a commercial license, does this mean that I, in some manner unknown, be able to fly my favorite airplane, a Boeing 747, from San Francisco to Paris inside the Heavenly Kingdom? Okay, I know this is a nutty question, but it's a good example of stretching what I believe are the Holy characteristics of the Heavenly realm. Yes, dear Lord, you can tease me all you want. I can hear you laughing already.

August 22, 2022, 11.20 AM
Answers from our Father in Heaven

1. *"Oh, my dear child, you have posed fascinating and pertinent questions to benefit our sacred children. Thank you for asking them about me. The answer to your question about advancing to higher levels when a child is already in the Heavenly Kingdom is undoubtedly yes. And yes, you are correct that your Father encourages working and learning more and more about yourself and everything around you. And learning, you will automatically increase your ability to love and help others of those in Heaven more deeply and thoroughly. This is by giving of yourself to all others of God's children. This will result in an ever-increasing reward for our children who put forth the effort.*

2. *Yes, my dear son, there are other forms of life within the created realms that your Father has done. However, they have no impact on your life and the trajectory of your existence. The best word to*

describe this is that you are separated from other life forms. This is a very good thing because knowing other forms of life necessarily means that you will be exposed to the knowledge of different sets. Exposed to the laws of physics, different situations that these other kinds of children of God are dealing with entirely separate from your own. Everything about any other kind of children of God is very foreign and almost always from your existence. Hence, there is no benefit for you to know anything about the other dimensions, the other forms of life. If you did know something, it would be detrimental to your Spiritual path back to us in The Trinity and especially your infinite loving Almighty Father.

3. *A Serious Warning. I should mention that over the recent past, there have been encounters with another form of life on the surface of the Earth. I mentioned earlier Satan is a multidimensional being because he is a fallen angel out of the Heavenly realm due to his rebellion long before your Heavenly Father decided to create His sacred children. Your habitation on Earth is sacred and has a sacred purpose of giving you the choice of whether you wish to return to the Heavenly Kingdom and the paradise that awaits you. Or, by how you conduct your lives on Earth, to choose Satan. Satan is very active on Earth and permeates our Heavenly Father's sacred children in so many ways that display themselves in the way people conduct their lives. It is that simple.*

There Are Some Rare Times in Which One Or More of God's Sacred Children Encounter What Is Called Extraterrestrial Beings. Stay Away from These Encounters, No Matter How Curious You Might Be. These Encounters and What You Would Call Spaceships or Flying Saucers Originate from Satan and The Dimension of Hell.

No Good Has Ever Come to Any of God's Sacred Children with Their Encounters of These Demonic Creatures. Every Incident Has Resulted in Some Form of Damage

To God's Sacred Children Due To the Hate of Satan. The People Who Closely Investigate These Encounters Are Putting Themselves at Great Risk of Demonic Damage to Themselves. They Are Bypassing the Normal Protection from Our Angels to Satisfy Their Dangerous Curiosities. Enough Said.

4. *Regarding the size of the Heavenly realm, it is true that the Heavenly realm has no boundaries. It encompasses and supersedes all other realms. It must be this way because the Holy Trinity has access to all realms and is present in every particle of existence and all realms. All of this points to the creation of a pathway for all of God's sacred children back to Him in the Heavenly Kingdom, which means their redemption. The Heavenly Kingdom is relatively small and has significantly fortified and protected boundaries around it in all directions. So that there cannot be even the slightest incursion that is not permitted by our very strict laws of entry.*

5. *First, this is a very profound question. It is fundamental to all existence. What The Trinity means by the word "life" and all of God's children is that there must be specific characteristics and attributes to a being that exists in the Spiritual and/or physical realms.*

   Within the Spiritual realm, abundant life is featured by a separate identity from all others. A separate life means an individual and separate will. A separate point of view when perceiving reality around it, being able to communicate with others of its kind as a separate entity and being perceived as a separate entity from others of its kind. There must be a certain minimum level of intelligence and reasoning power. There must be a memory, and it must follow specific rules of behavior that govern its actions in the environment in which it lives.

   Their life must be able to form relationships with others of its kind, participating in group activities but also having the ability to act alone. It must be sentient, absorbing information regarding its environment and other life forms. It must make decisions based on experience, memory, environmental information, instinct, and habit patterns. It must be able to act to preserve its own survival. These are a few of the characteristics that earmark a life in the physical realm. The Spiritual realm is different.

6. *Regarding the fact that our universe is designed where everything is completely visible, nothing can be hidden within all creation, this is the manner in which your Almighty Father decided to design all creation.*

Think of what it would be like if this were not true. Within the sphere of God's children or human life if there was no such thing as truth or having the natural flow be earmarked by unknown secrets, there would be no cultures there would be no societies, it would not be possible to have loving relationships because loving relationships are built on knowing the other person in detail.

There would always be rightful suspicion of anyone and everybody in all circumstances. Society would cease to function even in the most straightforward interpersonal transactions.

The human justice system is based on discovering what defendants are hiding and trying to keep secrets. Without the exposure of truth, there would be no justice in society, and victims of crime would not have any recourse against perpetrators who cause damage in one way or another. Simply put, there can be no secrets. The decision on judgment day is based upon knowing every little detail of each child of God. This means not only learning a person's actions but also the emotions, motivations, intentions, and other factors that play inside the Spirit and mind of the human person.

Almost everybody does not know or understand that within the human mind, there are no secrets from God. Absolutely everything is revealed and known by The Trinity. This is what is used to make a completely fair decision regarding the eternal future of every child of God. I love this question of yours, dear son.

Leave it to you to come up with an extremely entertaining yet complex example of the dimensionality of the Heavenly Kingdom. This tells me that you do understand how the Heavenly Kingdom exists within the Heavenly realm. I know that some of the happiest moments in your life on earth were in an airplane doing all sorts of things that only a very seasoned and experienced pilot could do.

The answer to your question is, of course, yes. For that matter, if you wish, you could take one of the airplanes you own and fly them to the moon. Remember, dear son, there are no limitations in the Heavenly Kingdom. Knowing you, I think you might even try that. It would give me great pleasure and joy to watch you do exactly that and many other things that will come from your delightful imagination."

Well, now I know in practical terms just how limitless the Heavenly Kingdom really is. If I can fly my airplane to the moon, then all sorts of other ideas also come to my mind. A good friend of mine, a very good friend, passed away, and I know he is in Heaven. I have **Damn it you stop it** with Him a few times since his death. He loves motorcycles. I imagine now he could take his motorcycle to the moon also.

Remember, dear Christian reader, although all this sounds nutty and ridiculous, these impractical examples serve to demonstrate just how limitless it is in God's Heavenly Kingdom for us, His sacred children. It is indeed a magnificent paradise for all eternity. In my magnificent conversations with our Lord and Savior, Jesus Christ, specifically told me that within the Heavenly Kingdom, there are no limitations. If you think about this, now you know the reason why our Heavenly Father demands that not one particle of sin is ever allowed within the gates of the Heavenly Kingdom. Think about it, dear reader.

Also, think about why when some of our Holy Father's sacred children choose not to be tested on earth and instead remain within the Heavenly Kingdom, there are certain restrictions eternally placed on them. And at the same time there is no stigma attached to their decision not to come to earth. It can be said accurately that their love for their Father in Heaven is so great that they do not want to risk anything that might interfere with that love for Him.

Just be faithful, dear Christian, be of good heart loving our creator knowing that in the not-too-distant future we will be within the Heavenly Kingdom living a life, an eternal life in paradise. We will have no limitations but also have the best loving guidance from The Trinity that we could ever imagine. It is not all harps and violins people. How about football games and baseball too?

16

The Character of Almighty God

This is a wonderful exercise for we are using our magnificent brain and consciousness and reasoning power that God has given us so we can know Him better than we have ever known Him before.

One BIG opportunity for learning about God is the character and nature of our Father in Heaven. One God? That idea was preposterous in the minds of people 2000 years ago. So, what are the attributes of our Christian God in Heaven? He is the one true and only God of all things seen and unseen, visible and invisible.

There is no other God but Him. That is the true Biblical view arrived at in the Bible. It was Abraham who was the first that introduced this truth to the Hebrew people ever so long ago, and since then, our understanding of God has expanded greatly since then. The following is a list of the attributes of our Heavenly Father and is listed in both the Old Testament and the New Testament.

The Biblical List of God's Attributes or Character [16], [17]

1. To begin with, regarding us, His children are made in His image. He is a loving Father to all believers. Ephesians 1:2; Galatians 1:1; Colossians 1:12; 1 Thessalonians 1:3.

2. God has emotions to some unknown degree. In the documented dialog in this book, our Father displayed emotions like "I am well pleased." I am sure this cannot be His only emotion. There must be others, like anger and love. But I must emphasize that I do not know for sure. He shows us His love for us and His children in so many ways, like creating the physical and Spiritual realms so we can return to Him. He talks about joy and fulfillment within The

---

[16] The Character of God Bible Study.doc (ocfusa.org)

[17] https://www.gotquestions.org

Trinity, etc. Other indicators are verses in the Bible and the fact that we, too, have emotions. Could we have emotions if our Father didn't? Yes, God does have emotions.

3. God has no beginning or end and is eternal. He always was, He is and always will be. *I know this to be true from personal experience. I one of my discussions with God, I asked Him how he created the physical realm and what did He create before our universe. He revealed to me in detail that I will tell you about later in this book.* Psalm 90:2; Genesis 1:1; Psalm 102:27

4. God Almighty is always faithful (Immutable) and unchanging in His promises and words. He can be trusted in all things because God Himself is truth. Remember what Jesus said, I am the way, the truth, and the life. No one can go to the Father except through me. *In my time with our Lord, everything, and I mean everything, He revealed to me down to the last detail, was and remains true. Even regarding things about my family that later turned out to be just like He said.* Hebrews 13:8; James 1:17; Malachi 3:6; Numbers 23:19; Psalm 102:26-27.

5. God's justice is perfect and fair. He is no respecter of persons meaning a lowly person in society is treated the same as one in high places. Good deeds will be rewarded, and evil will be punished. *One time I misspoke about something that God told me not to say. I forgot, and accidentally, I did what I was not supposed to do. Immediately, God told me as penance, I had to walk an extra three miles. I remember that until this day.* Deuteronomy 32:4; Psalm 19:9; Genesis 18:25.

6. Love is the very expression of His eternal identity and character. God is perfect love because He always seeks His perfect will in us and desires to see us in the center of His sacred and Holy will. He loves us so much that He sent His only begotten son to die and pay for our sins. John 3:16; 1 John 4-8, 16

7. Omniscience: God knows every detail of our existence. He knows every detail of everything we have ever done, what we are doing to the point that he even knows the number of hairs on our heads. He knows our thoughts and what we say. He has a perfect recall of all events in the past, no matter how large or small. *When God*

was with me about this book as I was writing it, he already knew its contents from what He told me in a story below. Yes, God does indeed know everything down to the last detail. It is impossible to have any secrets anywhere within God's loving creation and this is explained in multiple places within this book of love. When we were all born to earth, we did NOT leave our Heavenly Father. Rather we remained within the limitless spiritual realm that IS our Heavenly Father. Father IS always with us and NEVER apart from us.

8. Omnipotence: God has unlimited power. God is all-powerful. There is nothing too hard for Him.

   Jeremiah 32:17, 1 Peter 1:5 *From what God told me about how He created the Spiritual worlds and the two creations, He must be everything the Bible tells us about Him. More on this later.*

9. Omnipresence: God is everywhere. There is no place in Heaven, in the Spiritual realm, and on earth where He is not present. The apostle John said, "no matter where I go, God is there." God is also present in our hearts and in our minds. Even though many of us who are children of God are very uncomfortable with that thought and will deny the omnipresence of God. There is no place that God isn't. Psalm 139:7-12, 1 Kings 8:27.

   This is a thought that completely torments those that are of Satan for they want desperately to hide from our Heavenly Father and anybody who is directly associated with Almighty God. I have personally encountered and lost friends over this very phenomenon. In one case at my 75th birthday party, I was attacked with lies by the husband of a very good friend of mine of 45 years. The wife defended the lies of her husband, and I thus terminated our long-standing friendship. Nothing is more important than truth, for our Lord and Savior said that He is the way the truth and the life and nobody goes to the Father except by Him. The wife chose very badly.

10. Righteous: God is sinless, Holy, and perfect. All that He does is correct, right, and proper. He has no sinful nature and never violates His own Scripture. 1 Peter 1:15-16, 1 John 1:5, 1

Samuel 2:2, Deuteronomy 9:14, Psalm 99:9; Deuteronomy 32:4, Psalm 145:17

11. Sovereign: God is supreme with no one to answer to. He is completely independent and can make decisions without anyone else's agreement or consent. Isaiah 40:13-14, Deuteronomy 4:39, Ephesians 1

12. Truth: Everything that God says or does is the correct word or action for us to follow. He is ultimately "correct" in every situation. [18]Titus 1:2, Romans 3:4, Romans 11:33, Numbers 23:19

13. God knows about everything that is happening in your life. This is like number 8 above and includes every action and event that occurs in your life. There is nothing that God does not know about every one of His children. In a real sense we are part of God, and He is part of us. In this way, it is impossible for Father NOT to hear every prayer we say.

14. Our Heavenly Father Is Always concerned about our health and well-being. Exquisite and powerful healing processes are designed within our bodies that fight all things organic that would prematurely end our lives. See the next topic.

How To Talk Directly to Our Heavenly Father:

It is one thing to know God is omnipresent, but it is another thing to understand how to benefit from that. You as a Christian may talk to God directly at any time, day or night. It is impossible for God not to hear what you have to say. Nothing is too small for our loving Father. It is impossible for our Father not to be very interested in what you tell Him. God is ALWAYS with us every second of every day. There is NEVER an instant when His loving presence is not intimately close to us.

If something is bothering you, take what you have to say, make the sign of the cross, say one "Our Father and one Hail Mary." Do this in a quiet place with no possible interruptions. Then talk directly to our Father using your normal language. Then after you are done, ask Him to answer you now, not tomorrow or next week, etc. but right now. Ask Him to answer you now immediately after you finish praying. Frame your question or request with a gentle and respectful vocabulary.

Be humble. You are talking to Almighty God, who created absolutely everything around you, the whole universe, all that is seen and unseen. He created YOU! Then prepare yourself to hear His response in several different ways. Good books are written about this very topic. No time here for that now. On another note, ask God to allow you to feel His presence with you.

This is NOT scary stuff as many would imagine. Doing this gives me a great feeling of security and love that emanates from our Father. Ask Him to be close to you as if you both are standing side by side. He will always appear on your right side, never on the left. Remember the sheep and goats' story. Open your mind and rest in the image of His being right next to you. I would be very surprised if you did not feel His Divine peaceful presence. I have done this many times especially when I am feeling down about something. If you do not feel God's loving presence, then try again gently concentrating on relaxing first and slowly saying your two prayers.

You do not have to have a specific issue or problem to talk with our Father. Just say the two prayers above and say to God: "Hi God, I just wanted to greet you and tell you that I love you." God would love it if you did something like this. This is something that I personally do on a regular basis. Many times, I hear back from our loving Father in Heaven when he says, "I love you." Never be afraid of our loving Father in Heaven, for always remember that he is our personal creator, and he already resides within us. His voice is soft, loving, and clear, as I have heard many times.

Remember our Father IS a personal God that is indeed most interested in everything you have to say. Remember God is on your side. You are created in His image. He wants to hear from you and is never "too busy" to address whatever you have to say. I have done this many times and He sometimes answers within a second or two. Yup! He is that fast dear friend. Other times God might decide it's better for Him to answer your question later when the time is more right. Below is a true story of an incredible event that happened spontaneously one afternoon as I was writing a different section of this very book.

Almighty God is a very personal God.

One of the most beautiful aspects of creation, both physical and spiritual, is you and I are both physical and spiritual in our very nature that our Heavenly Father created unknown billions of years ago. The spiritual part of us can always be used to pray to Almighty God and talk with Almighty God. First, this means it is impossible for us to talk to God or pray to God without Him knowing exactly what it is we wish to say to Him. So many people have been taught that the sacred children of God are stuck on the physical earth and that their Heavenly Father is over there somewhere.

This is completely wrong and damaging. For God loves all his sacred children so very much that he left a part of Himself within our spiritual being. This is the way our Heavenly Father made sure that every one of his sacred children may speak with Him at any time for any reason. This duality of our existence was intended and created by The Trinity untold billions of years ago. Our Heavenly Father loves us so much that he provided this way so we can talk with Him and pray to Him no matter what the situation is.

I should note that all communication with the divine is telepathic. If you were standing next to me when I said a prayer to our Father or Jesus Christ, you would hear nothing. My dear wife Evangeline experiences this kind of thing with me quite often. Sometimes we will be talking and suddenly God would break in and tell me something about a topic I have been addressing in my mind. When this happens, my dear wife has no idea what occurred. I then must tell her something like, "oh, something just occurred to me I must write it down. I will be back."

This is just like when the Holy Golden Orb appeared to me on a jet over the Pacific Ocean. When the magnificent brightly lit Golden Orb appeared to me, all the other people in the jet with me saw nothing. That Holy appearance changed my life. Details on this mystic experience can be found in a book I wrote several years ago titled **"The Divine Resting on My Shoulder."**

An Unexpected Loving Encounter with Almighty God

This next page is a personal story of just one divine incident that happened to me without warning. This event occurred while I was working on a different section of this book. I was in my wife's recliner chair in our meditation room with my laptop computer. It was dark in this room with a few statuettes of the Crucifix, St. Joseph, and our Blessed Virgin Mary. I was not writing at that moment.

Rather, what was on my mind was some of the topics I was going to write about in the book you are reading now. While my thoughts were elsewhere, without any advance notice or warning, our Heavenly Father started communicating with me. Yes, He does these things according to His timing, not mine.

I think it is so comforting to me and wonderful that our Heavenly Father breaks into the flow of my life when he feels he wants to. I openly and lovingly welcome these instances and in many ways it's like a sigh of relief for me because it reassures me my Father in Heaven is with me every moment of my existence.

I again noticed His voice was one of a very loving and kind Father who was gently talking to one of His children. His voice was one of kindness and love. He tends to speak a little slowly. I like that, as I can understand every word he says. I felt very comforted in hearing from Him again.

This Is What Our Loving Almighty Father Revealed to Me That Afternoon: May 28, 2022

"What you have said so far in your book, I am very pleased. of what you have written so far regarding the creation of all that you can understand, I am also pleased. Ask my son for more details on all of that. Tell my children that I love them more than they can possibly imagine. To reassure them, tell them I am always with them as they imagine but also in other ways that they cannot.

You are the first that I am allowing to speak with me directly and let that be written. You are a unique child of mine and I am very pleased. Remind my children I am with them in every way. All the universe to the entire earth I crafted, so my children could live in the physical world and meet me to learn about me and come closer to me, which gives me great delight.

To create the earth and all before it that made it possible, it did not take what your scientists say about time. For me, it was what you would call a blink in time. You are correct that I live in so many dimensions that you cannot understand. I live within each of your bodies and every cell within. It is I that powers everything within your bodies to let you live within my loving graces for I do love you so much. Yes, I am in every cell of your body, and yes, I do know the number of hairs on your head. You will have a great sense of pleasure and joy once you finish your book. I love you very much, my dear son, and you know that I am with you in every way for all eternity.

They're signing themselves in the living room Yes, you are right that I created all my children at the same time. And before I created the Spiritual realm. Each of you is far different than you know, and each of you knows inwardly that I am your Father. Ask my son for more details about what I did and what we created before we created the Spiritual realm. And ask Him how all the realms relate to each other. I know this is what you want to hear. I know you better than you know yourself, and I know the questions that were coming to your mind. You have lived your life well and chose to put other people ahead of yourself. This is why I gifted you with being able to talk with me directly. This is special, and so are you. I love you for all eternity, as you will experience. <u>Lastly, do not cast your book before swine, and do not lower yourself to those who hate me and you.</u> I will talk to you again."

Our Father's revelation above flowed nicely into a speech file on my computer. After our Father finished the last sentence above, I was completely speechless. After He finished, I asked our Father if I got everything correct. He indicated that I did.

Hard To Believe, But True

I would understand if you had a hard time accepting the above as true. But we all must remember that the Bible is full of miracles like this. One example is the virgin birth of our Lord and Savior, Jesus of Nazareth. God can do anything that he chooses, with anybody choosing at any time you choose.

The reason I include this story is that it demonstrates just what I talked about regarding God's personal character. Think about it, dear child. Just how lucky we are to be children of such a loving Father in Heaven. Also, remember that our lord and Savior. There was nothing wrong with that question, but I think it's a question of the world. Jesus Christ showed His immense love for us by being born on earth as we are and then voluntarily died on the cross to vanquish our sins. Now we just need to love Almighty God in return and follow His rules for us as we live our lives.

I cannot forget the Holy Spirit also. He is always present and guides us as well. Additionally, he urges us to pray and always nudges us to keep a good Christian life. Blessed Mother Mary is such a loving woman and expresses her great love for me in different ways. Speaking of our Blessed Mother Mary, next is a story about her and me on the freeway.

Our Blessed Mother Mary Always Is Watching Over Me.

Even on the freeway, she is protecting me from myself. This is an embarrassing story about when I was driving my 500-hp Corvette on the freeway in California. It was a bad traffic situation I found myself in where a bunch of cars were close together, constantly getting in each other's way and making aggressive lane changes only a very few feet apart. For my own personal physical safety, I needed to get the heck out of there, so I had to "punch it "to get away from them. It took only about three seconds and then I was going from 60 MPH to more than 100 mph to get away from some of the crazy drivers that are now far behind me. I escaped to an opening in the traffic far ahead. Now I was safe. No more rubbing door panels with angry drivers. Now! As I was accelerating, suddenly, I heard our Blessed Mother Mary say to me, "My son! SLOW DOWN! SLOW DOWN! SLOW DOWN!

After a while, when I got back home, I thought about what happened. I then realized that there I was, driving down the freeway in my car taking evasive action using the monster power that my Corvette must escape from crazy drivers. <u>Then there I was, getting scolded by Mother Mary in Heaven</u>. Talk about connections, WOW! Think about this, dear Christian friend. Mother Mary was with me all the time and could hold back no longer her concern for my safety and how fast I went. She, too, works to protect us, even from ourselves.

I realized that our Blessed Mother Mary was not able to perceive why I did what I did to protect myself from the idiots that were driving recklessly so close to me. One of the advantages of driving such a powerful sports car was the evasive capabilities that it had to get away from other reckless drivers so close to me. It could accelerate into an open spot in traffic where they could not get to me. I always feel that if you are far away from other cars, they cannot hit you.

Perhaps this story gives a stronger hint to you, dear child, of just how much we are truly loved by The Trinity and, of course, our Blessed Mother Mary. Cherish this story, dear Christian, for it is completely true. Our Blessed Mother Mary is always watching over us in this concern with love in her heart every moment of every day. Remember this story always, dear Christian. This is true even in a very powerful Corvette sports car.

17

Our Heavenly Father's Loving Ten Commandments & Three Rules of Life

Your Author's Commentary:

It is Almighty God, as expressed by the members of The Trinity — our Almighty Father, our Lord and Savior Jesus Christ, and the Holy Spirit —which brings order, Fairness, and equality into all creation. It is these three Holy and infinite Gods that bring us all that is seen and unseen. Each of them is infinite in all ways. It is correct to say that The Trinity is three infinite loving Gods expressed as one yet also one Almighty God Expressed as three.

From experience in writing eleven sacred books that complement our Holy Bible, it is my pure and perfect testimony each of the three in The Trinity is different from the other two. Especially in personality and the role they play in all creation.

Summing up the reason for having appropriate rules of existence for all creation, it would be without these rules of life and the Ten Commandments the creation, everything seen and unseen would destroy itself. The destruction of all creation is the exact goal of Satan, who rebelled against our Heavenly Father. Within the blink of an eye, Satan and his demons were kicked out of the Heaven to dwell in a small space of the spiritual realm called hell and a small planet called Earth.

Most all, most of our Heavenly Fathers wanted to come to Earth to volunteer to take what is known as the" earth test." This is what you and I are doing right now. All of us sacred children on Earth are here to take a very profound test. It is a simple choice in measuring our love for our Heavenly Father. Do we accept our loving Almighty Father? Or do we reject Him? We answer this question by the way we lead our lives while on Earth. In essence, do we follow the 10 Commandments and our Father's three overarching rules for our life? Or not?

The Ten Commandments

First are the 10 Commandments. It is so very sorrowfully unfortunate that very many people treat Father's 10 commandments as "The 10 Suggestions". Doing that is yet another way of rejecting Almighty God because the sacred child that thinks this way is putting themselves higher than our Heavenly Father.

Aside from that, I present the Godly Rules of Behavior in two separate ways. The original way was given to Moses, and then the comprehensive way in a summary manner that requires a much deeper understanding of the original 10 commandments.

One thing I must say is that if the 10 Commandments are followed, they will result in far happier lives and much greater contentment and love among all people on Earth. The increase in happiness and fulfillment in a person's life that results from following the 10 Commandments is indeed much greater. There will be far less controversy and heartache by living your life according to God's sacred 10 commandments. These commandments are actually a magnificent gift to all of our Heavenly Father's children on earth because they bring, as said earlier, an excellent way of living that reduces conflict and other negativity that would otherwise be present If they were not followed.

When I was a little boy growing up and in the first and second grades, I thought to myself, great, now I have even more and more rules that I have to live according to. It's bad enough that my Father was a strict and cruel authoritarian who would punish me for the slightest little thing that he thought I did wrong. Now I got "that big guy in the sky" looking down at me, commanding me to do this and to do that, not to do this and not to do that such that my whole life is nothing more than a bunch of rules that can only bring nothing but punishments for this and punishments for that.

It took a very long time growing up before I began to understand the magnificent beauty of the 10 Commandments and, even more importantly, frankly, the three summary Rules of Life that will lead people into the Heavenly Kingdom.

The 10 Commandments [19]

1. *"I am the LORD your God, who brought you out of the land of Egypt, out of the house of bondage. You shall have no other gods before Me."* (Exodus 20:2-3)

2. *"You shall not make for yourself a carved image—any likeness of anything that is in Heaven above, or that is in the earth beneath, or that is in the water under the earth; you shall not bow down to them nor serve them. For I, the LORD your God, am a jealous God, visiting the iniquity of the Fathers upon the children to the third and fourth generations of those who hate Me, but showing mercy to thousands, to those who love Me and keep My commandments."* (Exodus 20:4-6)

3. *"You shall not take the name of the LORD your God in vain, for the LORD will not hold Him guiltless who takes His name in vain."* (Exodus 20:7)

4. *"Remember the Sabbath day, to keep it Holy. Six days you shall labor and do all your work, but the seventh day is the Sabbath of the LORD your God. In it you shall do no work: you, nor your son, nor your daughter, nor your male servant, nor your female servant, nor your cattle, nor your stranger who is within your gates. For in six days the LORD made the Heavens and the earth, the sea, and all that is in them, and rested the seventh day. Therefore the LORD Blessed the Sabbath day and hallowed it."* (Exodus 20:8-11)

---

[19] The 10 Commandments: Full List, Bible Verses and Meaning (christianity.com)

5. *"Honor your Father and your Mother, that your days may be long upon the land which the LORD your God is giving you."* (Exodus 20:12)

6. *"You shall not murder."* (Exodus 20:13)

7. *"You shall not commit adultery."* (Exodus 20:14)

8. *"You shall not steal."* (Exodus 20:15)

9. *"You shall not bear false witness against your neighbor."* (Exodus 20:16)

10. *"You shall not covet your neighbor's house; you shall not covet your neighbor's wife, nor His male servant, nor His female servant, nor His ox, nor His donkey, nor anything that is your neighbor's."* (Exodus 20:17)

One thing regarding the physical creation of the universe and the creation of all of our Heavenly Father's sacred children is that every one of us, because our Heavenly Father created us in His image, also has left part of Himself deep within our Spiritual being. This manifests itself in an inner sense of what is right and wrong. Our conscience other words! Every small child exhibits the presence of a fundamental understanding of right and wrong as guided by Our Heavenly Father, who loved us so much that he left part of Himself within our spiritual being. We see this in one and two-year-old babies where if someone takes a toy from them, they cry because inwardly, they already know that it is wrong. We all have a sense of love inborn within us. When we look at our Mothers and Fathers, we smile. That is the way a baby demonstrates their inner love. Babies frequently make loving sounds like cooing or giggling when they are held by a parent who loves them.

Babies born into this world have part of Heaven still within them because they are only about one year away from the Heavenly realm from where they came. Nobody ever thinks of this, but what I just said is true. Look for the story about my first granddaughter when I was propelled into the Heavenly nursery, where she was preparing herself for being born to Earth within the subsequent three months.

Our Heavenly God's 10 commandments, as brought forth by Moses, are precisely what the Hebrews needed to behave by and lead our lives in that manner. However, there is another way to look at our Heavenly Father's commands for us to live by. It is the following three rules of life for each and every one of us.

Our Heavenly Father's 3 Behavioral Rules of Life

There is another way of Conducting our sacred lives on Earth that will certainly help us return to the Heavenly Kingdom. These three rules of life Can be thought of as an expression of the Ten Commandments in a different way that guides us to a manner in which we can behave in the social environment in which we live.

I suppose it simplifies things in that there are only three things to remember instead of 10. However, the 10 Commandments are more comprehensive, so it would be excellent for every Christian, a sacred child of God, to be very knowledgeable about both.

1. Throughout Your Life, <u>Always Love Almighty God first above everything</u> else.

    This is ever so important. Please remember that our Almighty Father is the source of all life and the source of all three realms of existence: the spiritual realm, the physical realm, and our physical bodies, which enable us to take the Earth Test, so we may return to the Heavenly Kingdom.

    This may sound harsh, but it is not. When the above sentences talk about always love almighty God first above everything else, <u>the words "above everything else "mean exactly that!"</u> No sacred child of God should ever put anything else above their relationship with our heavenly father and creator of all that is seen and unseen. This means that every other human being in your life <u>is secondary to your relationship with Almighty God.</u> This means every member of your family is necessarily secondary to our heavenly Father, our lord and savior Jesus Christ and the Holy Spirit which precedes from them.

Every sacred child of God must always focus on the fact that it is our heavenly Father that has created every particle of their existence with no exceptions. Do not ever feel that in some way this is The Trinity forcing themselves down your throat. In another section of this book, it is outlined very clearly that for each sacred child of God to fulfill their earthly mission where each child is and always will be part of the existential relationship all of God's sacred children must put God ahead of everything else within their personal existence.

Remember," you have agreed to come to Earth for the "Earth Test". Putting other things on Earth ahead of Almighty God is a guarantee of failing the earth test which will send you directly to hell.

Lastly always remember that <u>no one goes to heaven except by our lord and savior Jesus Christ!</u> Be sure to concentrate on the next section titled, "no one goes to heaven except by Jesus Christ."

2. <u>Love others as you love yourself</u>. It is love, peace, understanding, and acceptance that bind and unite all of God's children while we are in the physical realm.
When I was growing up in the 1950's, this was called, "<u>The Golden Rule.</u>"
3. Love your enemies as you love yourself! This may sound redundant to number two above, but it is not. Your first reaction to this number three may be negative and think to yourself that loving your enemies is impossible. It is not. Please consider the life and times of our Lord and Savior Jesus Christ. He serves as the most holy example of what each and every one of us Christians need to follow.

18

It is only through Jesus Christ that we go to heaven!

In many ways this is the most important part of all Biblical Literature in the New Testament.

John 14:6 No One Comes to the Father Except Through Me.

Said differently, every sacred child of God while here on Earth taking the Earth test must have our lord and savior Jesus Christ at the top of their lives while we are here. It is ever so important that every child must have Jesus Christ as the center of their lives. If not, then they should not expect to enter into the heavenly kingdom upon their death.

The Fatal Fallacy of Good Works Only!

One of the most common deceptions by Satan is to lead people believe that if they are:

1. Good people
2. Do not sin too much
3. They are good neighbors in the community
4. Help others in need
5. People like them in the community
6. They are friendly and popular
7. They attend church regularly and give donations when the basket circulates at Mass

And the list goes on!

Good Works Alone Do Not Get You Back into Heaven

Everyone of God's sacred children Who come here for the earth test Must incorporate Our Lord and savior Jesus Christ into their lives. Talk to our Lord Jesus Christ. Think about our lord and savior Jesus Christ. Ask Jesus Christ questions about what you should do within your life when a situation confronts you.

Do you not know that almighty God which is also Jesus Christ by a different name knows every thought and every emotion and everything else within you? Nothing can ever be hidden! Jesus loves each of us so very much that he lives his infinite life within each of us and yearns to help us in every way possible. If you as a sacred child of God refuse Him, when your time comes that will balance out to you being refused to enter into the Heavenly Kingdom because you have demonstrated that is what you want.

It is for those people who refuse to have Jesus play in active role in their lives they will hear the following 4 terrible words upon their demise on Earth.

I Never Knew You

Why must all of us good Christian sacred children of Almighty God, always include our lord and savior Jesus Christ? The answer to this question is extremely simple and obvious once you pay attention to who Jesus Christ is. Jesus Christ is exactly what his title says he is. He is our lord that governs our activities and our proper thoughts while we were here on Earth and when we succeed in returning to the heavenly kingdom.

He is also our Savior. Savior from what? He is our loving savior that has redeemed us from automatically going to hell with no chance of returning to the Heavenly Kingdom. Lord and Savior Jesus Christ loves us so very very much that all he asks from us is to recognize who he is and cherish a relationship with him in our everyday lives we live on this earth during our earth test and beyond when we return to the heavenly kingdom.

If you include our lord and savior Jesus Christ within your day to day lives, you will experience the most magnificent and beautiful blessings that you could ever imagine. 2000 years ago Jesus died on a painful cross to redeem us all from hell. All we need to do is to include him in our daily lives and he will be with us always and forever more. He will answer any of our questions and bless us as we continue to take the earth test so we may return back to the heavenly kingdom with our lord and savior and experience life eternal like we even cannot imagine while we were here.

19

What Is Life?
Where Did Life Come From?

A Vital Part of this book.

This is a remarkably simple three-word question, yet it is profoundly complex. The answer to this question spans absolutely every facet of what we call life as human beings. The ultimate essence of life, in general, spans beyond humanity into other creations and the life contained within them as created by our Heavenly Father. I won't say any more about our Heavenly Father's other creations, as it would do nobody any good. Our Lord and Savior, Jesus Christ, has told me that multiple times. Possessing knowledge of other forms of life can do great damage to our Heavenly Father's sacred children. Yes! Knowledge of this kind can do great damage to you. <u>Stay very far away from extraterrestrial beings or non-human creatures.</u>

The Clear Definition

"All life is an extension of our loving Almighty Father.

Life in and of itself is each a separate and unique expression of our Heavenly Father.

Every life is a unique extension of our Father with its own separate free will and characteristics

For our Holy Father is the ultimate source of all that exists without exception."

It is unlimited love Emanating from Our Father that Holds all aspects of every creation in both animate and inanimate

There is no place in all creation where our Heavenly Father is not.

Said differently:

There Is but Only One Sacred Life-Only One! The center of all life forms as they are brought forth by our Almighty Father.

There Is Nothing in Existence Now And for evermore That Is Outside

Our Heavenly Sacred and Holy Trinity.

Said Differently, Which Is

Our Heavenly Almighty Father His Only Begotten Son Jesus Christ, And Our Holy Spirit. Everything, All Forms of Life Are Within The Life That Is Brought Forth from Our Almighty Father in Heaven.

There Is No Other Source of Life in Existence.

This Even Includes All the Other Creations That You Have Heard About in Other Sections of This Book. This is why love is the overwhelming force that brings all existence together. Love is in and of itself the binding force that brings together all aspects of life in existence.

Magnificent, Beautiful Thoughts of Godly Truth

1. There is only one life throughout all existence.
2. Our Heavenly Father is pure and perfect and infinite in all ways.
3. That single life is Almighty God.
4. All other lives are loving extensions of our Almighty Father.
5. All life in this creation and all other creations is an extension of our Heavenly Father.
6. All forms of life in this creation are a unique expression of our Almighty Father.
7. Nothing in this creation or others is separate from our loving Almighty Father.

8. The spiritual realm, the physical, and the laws of physics are also loving extensions of our Heavenly Father.

9. All the different physical dimensions, such as time, are also expressions of our loving Almighty Father.

10. All things seen or unseen are part of our Heavenly Father. He created it all.

11. Our Heavenly Father is pure and perfect and infinite in all ways.

12. Our Heavenly Father has created all physical laws for the benefit of His sacred children on earth.

13. Without our Heavenly Father, nothing would exist, both physically and unseen.

14. Heaven exists. I was once there and saw my future dwelling.

15. In some ways, all things that exist relate to all other things that exist. Why? Because everything is connected to our Heavenly Father.

16. Everything in existence is connected to every other thing by means of the Holy Spirit and the Magnificent Force of unrestricted love.

17. In many ways, love holds the entire universe together.

Your author strongly suggests that you review the above 17 points of meditation and study. The more you understand the foundational elements within this book, written mostly by our Lord and Savior Jesus Christ, the closer you will become to Almighty God.

20

The Loving Divine Unity of All Life and Existence

Jesus Christ
April 10, 2025

Everything within creation exists from and is part of Almighty God. Another way to look at this is quite simple. If it exists, the ultimate source of its existence is from our Heavenly Father, our Almighty Father. It is our Heavenly Father who is the source of all that is within the physical realm and all that is within the Spiritual realm. There are no exceptions whatsoever. Additionally, this is not a case where God created everything and then removed Himself to observe and see what happens.

The opposite is true. Our Heavenly Father is within every particle of existence, whether Spiritual or physical. This is especially true regarding His sacred beloved children who are created in His image — both you and me. We are very special creations for several reasons.

1. We are the only ones that are made in the image of our Heavenly Father. Have you ever noticed that regardless of how many years have passed, you still feel like yourself, not physically but from your self-identity, which gains wisdom and knowledge along the way?

2. We are temporary physical beings. However, due to the physical forces scientists call entropy and what Jesus Christ calls the law of disintegration, our physical bodies will last for only a relatively brief time. Then they stop functioning, and our Spiritual selves continue onward in their eternal life. When you wake up in the morning and look in the mirror, you might see a new itty-bitty wrinkle on your face or a new gray hair that you have not noticed

before. It is these kinds of things that emerge over time, providing direct evidence of entropy or the law of disintegration.

3. We are permanently Spiritual beings also made within the image of our Heavenly Father. It is our Spiritual beings that live onward for all eternity. This is with one exception. That exception is only if a sacred child of God rejects our loving Heavenly Father. And those that live their life in a way that proves beyond a doubt that they do reject our Heavenly Father's rules of existence and life. The way a sacred child lives their life is proof positive testimony that reveals whether they love our Heavenly Father or not. All the evidence resides within the tapestry of our lives.

4. Because we are both Spiritual and physical beings, the Spiritual part of us is highly connected with the Heavenly realm. This means our Heavenly Father, our Lord and Savior Jesus Christ, the Holy Spirit, which proceeds outward from them, and even our Blessed Mother Mary.

5. The Spiritual part of us is enormously wonderful. Why? It is because when each of us were created in the blink of an eye, our Heavenly Father loved us each so very much that he left part of Himself within us. This means that it is never ever a case of you being here and God being way over there somewhere else. No! Our Heavenly Father is not only within every particle of what he created but he is also within every one of our Spiritual bodies.

It is impossible for our Heavenly Father not to hear every one of our prayers. It is also impossible for our Heavenly Father not to be totally aware of everything that we say, everything that we do, everything that we think, everything that we feel, and so on. It is in this way The Trinity knows completely every tiny aspect of our entire lives and everything we experience and everything that we feel. It is in this way that it is impossible for Almighty God not to hear every one of our prayers no matter how insignificant it may seem to us.

This is also true when it comes to the moments after our physical bodies pass away. Our Heavenly Father is loving, he is just, and fair. It is in this way that each of our destinations, Heaven or hell will be determined from a pure and perfect perspective. Most people on the street when you ask them whether they believe in God or not, most will tell you they're not sure. If they say they believe in God, then they really do not understand much of anything about who God is and how he plays a vital role in their lives.

Usually, people think of God in terms of spatial distance between themselves and God living somewhere else up high in Heaven somehow. People believe that God is up high somewhere, and Satan is under the ground somewhere and we human beings are somehow stuck in the middle on the surface of the Earth. But that's about it. Fundamentally, people are exceedingly ignorant about the one true God that Christians know quite a bit about. Yet even with Christians they do not fully understand just how Almighty God is within us and around us. This is because most Christians do not give the Holy Trinity much thought.

The best way to understand all the different facets of existence both Spiritual and physical is to think of both everything as being intertwined together with our Almighty Father at its very center.

Almighty God is everywhere both in terms of the Spiritual realm and the physical realm. St Peter said in one of the psalms that no matter where he went our Heavenly Father was already there.

So, the very quick answer, to the question, "What Is Life" You simply answer by saying all life proceeds from our Heavenly Father and goes outward from Him and in its various forms. From this moment on I know that our Lord and savior Jesus Christ has several. Stop it damn your hinges, he wants to emphasize to all of you and I want our Lord to add to anything that I just said.

What is the ultimate origin of our life?

We know that we are not a collection of accidental chemicals that, over time, somehow came together to form our physical bodies. That is complete and utter elementary school nonsense. There is no secular explanation of where our bodies come from, and certainly NOT where spiritual bodies come from either. Dr. Hugh Ross is one of my favorite authors and has dedicated his life to sharing God's truth and explaining God's handiwork in creating everything that exists, which includes you and me. Hugh Ross books - Google Search

Does anyone think that Charles Darwin had the Magic Formula many decades ago for where our bodies come from? If anybody believes that, they are sadly mistaken. I bet many of them don't realize if they believe that hogwash Darwinian interpretation, they also are automatically denying the existence of Almighty God and denying the very source of their own existence.

It is incredible that some people are so ignorant and gullible. They believe a botanist who worked for a few months in the Galapagos Islands produced a theory explaining that human life is just beyond anything that has the slightest tendency of intelligence to it. Now, I am not a Darwin hater by any means. In fact, I consider him to be a very good scientist and botanist. In his book The Origin of Species, he said if it can be shown that changes in a species over a long period cannot be explained then my theory is wrong. I recommend his book to anybody, frankly.

Human beings have two magnificent parts to them. One is, of course, our physical body. The second one is far more important, and that is our spiritual body. Our physical body can only last from 70 to 90 years before significant portions of it stop working and it dies. However, our spiritual bodies continue to exist for all eternity. Other sections in this book explain this in detail.

All life originates from Our Heavenly Almighty Father. Yes! All life, no matter what form it takes. When it comes to our Heavenly Father's sacred children, He loved us so much. So much that when he loved us into existence that He left inside of our spiritual selves part of his own consciousness, part of Himself. It is accurate to say our Heavenly Father, Lord Jesus Christ, and the Holy Spirit do love us. So much that they participate without us knowing it; they participate in our lives, our love, our struggles, our worries and everything else. We're inseparable from them, and they are inseparable from us.

I will give you just one example. When I was writing the book titled **"God's Grand Design: Blessed Mother Mary Speaks, Her Apparitions, The End of Times."** Mother Mary is with me constantly, and as I was writing this book, she was ever so close to me. And when I came up with some descriptions of things, the Blessed Mother Mary was right there, suggesting how to phrase them and their content.

The title of the book that Mother Mary and I co-wrote together is **God's Grand Design, Blessed Mother Mary Speaks of Her Apparitions, And the End of Times**. Now, frequently, because of documenting the horrific events coming our way during the End of Times, I would get quite upset just visualizing the awful suffering that will happen to people living on Earth. I never said anything, but Blessed Mother Mary knew I was getting very upset, and she offered to, on a few occasions, stop the writing process for a while so I could recover my emotions. Yes, my dear sacred child of God, we are indeed that close to each other. She is in Heaven, and I am on Earth.

Yet, I will tell you something else about my existence. Yes, in detail in another one of my books. I cannot begin to explain to you just how lucky I am.

For the last number of years, both our Lord and Savior Jesus Christ and our Blessed Mother Mary have been with me no more than 12 inches away from my left and right shoulders. This is something that will continue until I return to the Heavenly Kingdom. Also, every word I write whether from our Heavenly Father or our Blessed Mother Mary or the Holy Spirit and Our Lord Jesus Christ is always scrutinized word for word by our Lord Savior Jesus Christ.

We can speak to each other any time we wish about anything we want. This is because I am our Almighty Father's Anointed Messenger. This is all I want to say for now.

Everything within creation exists from and is part of Almighty God. Another way to look at this is quite simple. If it exists, the ultimate source of its existence is from our Heavenly Father, our Almighty Father. It is our Heavenly Father who is the source of all that is within the physical realm and all that is within the Spiritual realm. There are no exceptions whatsoever. Additionally, this is not a case where God created everything and then removed Himself to observe and see what happens.

The opposite is true. Our Heavenly Father is within every particle of existence, whether it be Spiritual or physical. This is especially true regarding His sacred beloved children who are created in His image. This is both you and me. We are very special creations for several reasons.

1. We are the only ones that are made in the image of our Heavenly Father.

2. We are temporary physical beings. However, due to the physical forces scientists call entropy. and what Jesus Christ calls the law of disintegration; our physical bodies will last for only a brief time. Then they stop functioning, and our Spiritual selves continue onward in their eternal life. When you wake up in the morning and look in the mirror, you might see a new itty-bitty wrinkle on your face or a new gray hair that you have not noticed before. It is these kinds of things that emerge over time, providing direct evidence of entropy or the law of disintegration. Have you ever noticed that regardless of how many years have passed by you still feel like yourself, not physically but from your self-identity which gains wisdom and knowledge along the way?

3. We are permanently Spiritual beings also made within the image of our Heavenly Father. It is our Spiritual beings that live onward for all eternity. This is with one exception. That exception is only if a sacred child of God rejects our loving Heavenly Father. And they live their life in a way that proves beyond a doubt that they do reject

our Heavenly Father's rules of existence and life. The way a sacred child lives their life is proof positive testimony that reveals whether they love our Heavenly Father or not. All the evidence resides within the tapestry of our lives.

Within this book, I have made significant efforts to show the different categories of people on the earth split up in many ways. I do this so you can get an excellent idea of the chances of various kinds of people going to Heaven or not.

4. Because we are both Spiritual and physical beings, the Spiritual part of us is highly connected with the Heavenly realm. This means our Heavenly Father, our Lord and Savior Jesus Christ, the Holy Spirit, which proceeds outward from them, and even our Blessed Mother Mary.

5. The Spiritual part of us is enormously wonderful. Why? It is because when each of us were created in the blink of an eye, our Heavenly Father loved us each so very much that he left part of Himself within us. This means that it is never ever a case of you being here and God being way over there somewhere else. No! Our Heavenly Father is not only within every particle of what he created but he is also within every one of our Spiritual bodies.

It is impossible for our Heavenly Father not to hear every one of our prayers. It is also impossible for our Heavenly Father not to be totally aware of everything that we say, everything that we do, everything that we think, everything that we feel, and so on. It is in this way The Trinity knows completely every tiny aspect of our entire lives and everything we experience and everything that we feel. It is in this way that it is impossible for Almighty God not to hear every one of our prayers no matter how insignificant it may seem to us.

This is also true when it comes to the moments after our physical bodies pass away. Our Heavenly Father is loving, he is just, and fair. It is in this way that each of our destinations, Heaven or hell will be determined from a pure and perfect perspective.

Most people on the street when you ask them whether they believe in God or not most will tell you they're not sure. If they say they believe in God, then they really do not understand much of anything about who God is and how he plays a vital role in their lives.

Usually, people think of God in terms of spatial distance between themselves and God living somewhere else up high in Heaven somehow. People believe that God is up high somewhere, and Satan is under the ground somewhere and we human beings are somehow stuck in the middle on the surface of the Earth. But that's about it. Fundamentally people are exceedingly ignorant about the one true God that Christians know quite a bit about. Yet even with Christians they do not fully understand just how Almighty God is within us and around us. This is because most Christians do not give the Holy Trinity much thought.

The best way to understand the different facets of existence, both spiritual and physical, is to think of everything as being intertwined together with our Almighty Father at its very center.

Almighty God is everywhere both in terms of the Spiritual realm and the physical realm. St Peter said in one of the psalms that no matter where he went our Heavenly Father was already there.

So, the very quick answer, to the question, "What Is Life" You simply answer by saying all life proceeds from our Heavenly Father and goes outward from Him and in its various forms. From this moment, I know our Lord and savior Jesus Christ has several things he wants to emphasize to all of you and I want our Lord to add to anything that I just said.

One thing everyone must remember is very important. When I say that our Heavenly Father created everything, that is exactly what I mean with no exception. Our Heavenly Father created all the mammals. He created all the birds in the sky. He created all the reptiles. He created all the foliage and all the flowers. He did this so all the animals on the land could eat heartily. He created all the fish in the sea and all the other animals in the sea so there would be an equilibrium between the different types. And they receive the necessary nourishment, including the mammals in the sea like whales and so on. Our Heavenly Father created The Four Seasons our beloved Earth experiences so for all the mammals and all the birds and all the other species will have food to eat.

As humans always like to do, they tend to focus just on human beings alone and nothing more as if we are the center of the universe. In many ways that is exactly who we are because the second member of The Trinity, Jesus Christ, sacrificed his life so all of God's sacred children could turn to Him within the Heavenly Kingdom.

Our Heavenly Father also created extraterrestrial planets and moons to keep the Earth in its proper orbit around the sun and ensure that the long-term solar and planetary cycles remain in a stable situation. Our Heavenly Father created the Milankovitch cycles, which over a long period of time regulates the Earth's orbit around the sun. Where, for a time, it oscillates to where there's a time when it's cold. This keeps things in balance on Earth.

Jesus Christ told me not too long ago that the favorable cosmic cycles that directly affect our Earth and its orbit in all its planetary seasons will start to degrade rapidly in approximately 105 years. Now this is not like turning on a light bulb. It is more like turning on a light with a rheostat. I suggest what is the ultimate origin of our life.

We know that we are not a pile of accidental chemicals that, over time, bumping into each other somehow formed our physical bodies. That is complete and utter nonsense. There is no secular explanation of where our bodies come from, and certainly NOT where our spiritual bodies come from either. Does anyone think that Charles Darwin had the Magic Formula many decades ago for where our bodies come from? If anybody believes that they are sadly mistaken. I bet many of them don't realize if they believe that hogwash, Darwinian interpretation, they also are automatically denying the existence of Almighty God and denying the very source of their own existence.

It's incredible that some people are so ignorant and gullible they believe a botanist produced a theory that explains all human life is just beyond anything that has the slightest tendency of intelligence to it. Now, I am not a Darwin hater by any means. In fact, I consider Him to be a very good scientist and botanist. In his book The Origin of the Species, he said that the changes in a species over time cannot be explained by a sequence of many minor changes, then my theory is wrong. I recommend his book to anybody, frankly.

Human beings have two magnificent parts to them. One is, of course, our physical body. The second one is far more important, and that is our spiritual body. Our physical body can only last from 70 to 90 years before major portions of it stop working and it dies. However, our spiritual body keeps on existing for all eternity. Other sections in this book explain this in detail.

All life originates from Our Heavenly Almighty Father. Yes! All life, no matter what form it takes. When it comes to our Heavenly Father's sacred children, our Heavenly Father when he loved us into existence that He left inside of our spiritual selves part of his own consciousness, part of Himself. It is accurate to say our Heavenly Father, Lord Jesus Christ, and the Holy Spirit do indeed love us so much they participate without us knowing it. They participate in our lives, our love, our struggles, our worries and everything else. We're inseparable from them, and they are inseparable from us.

I will give you one example. When I was writing the book titled God's Grand Design, Blessed Mother Mary Speaks, Her Apparitions, The End of Times. Mother Mary was with me constantly, and as I was writing this book, she was ever so close to me. And when I came up with some descriptions of things, Blessed Mother Mary was right there suggesting how to phrase things and the content of them.

The title of that book that Mother Mary and I co-wrote together is God's Grand Design, Blessed Mother Mary Speaks of Her Apparitions and The End of Times. Now, frequently, because of documenting the horrific events coming our way at the End of Times, I would get quite upset just visualizing the awful suffering that will happen to people living on Earth. I never said anything, but Blessed Mother Mary knew I was getting very upset, and she offered to, on a few occasions, stop the writing process for a while so I could recover my emotions. Yes, my dear sacred child of God, we are indeed that close to each other. She is in Heaven, and I am Father's Anointed Messenger on Earth.

Yet, I will tell you something else about my personal existence. For the last number of years, both our Lord and Savior Jesus Christ and our blessed Mother Mary have been no more than 12 inches away from my left shoulder and my right shoulder. We can speak to each other any time we wish about anything we want. This is because I am our Almighty Fathers Anointed Messenger. This is all I want to say for now.

This is a remarkably simple three-word question, yet it is a profoundly complex one that only a select few can even begin to answer. ***What Is Life?***! If you think you know the answer to this question, you don't. Below are a few samples of scientific answers that get nowhere in answering that easy three-word question.

Godly beauty within a sacred orb over the Pacific Ocean

Something unbelievable and magnificent happened to me on a jet halfway across the Pacific Ocean. This entire Sacred happening is discussed in  one of my previous books titled, "God Resting On My Shoulder" I was sitting in my usual window seat watching the water and clouds go by. Without warning, a beautiful, magnificent golden orb appeared above the aisle in the jet one row in front of me. It was ever so bright, emitting magnificently gorgeous rays of beautiful golden light in all directions. The picture is a pretty good illustration of what this magnificent orb looked like. It Was Pulsating as If It Was Alive. It Stayed There for A While and Then It Said These Words To Me, "God Loves You!" That was all. I was in my late 20s when this happened. The warmth, the tingling, and the love that the Golden Orb sent to me on that day have been with me ever since.

I have experienced other such divine events like this when I was delivering healing energy as a Reiki master later as well. This heralded the beginning of my ever-increasing Spiritual life with the sacred Trinity that would grow to magnificent intensity and love as my life continued onward.

My Personal Covenant of Truth with Almighty God

Quite some time ago, <u>I entered into a covenant of truth with our Heavenly Father</u>. By then, I had written several Spiritual books. It became very clear I entered a position that demanded I always tell the gospel truth of absolutely everything in all my books and my life. I promised our Heavenly Father that I would suffer under the pain of God's punishment if I ever did not.

The information in this book is sorely needed within the Christian community and all His sacred children. At this time in the history of mankind, we have never seen so much perversion, so much hostility, so much outright lies, and Satanic influence throughout all layers of society.

The situation today is very much that of the Sanhedrin in Jerusalem 2,000 years ago, attacking our Lord and Savior Jesus Christ. They felt very threatened, so they illegally had crucified Him. Only today, hatred against Almighty God and Christians is institutionalized within the structure of our American society, our entertainment industry, our news media, advertising industry. Everything is now censored to rid our culture in America of the truth of things if it does not fit into the liberal agenda of tyrannical socialism.

My Divine Purpose:

Our Holy Father has asked me to write His exact thoughts and words that contain extensive new knowledge of Christianity. It is designed completely for God's sacred children on earth today in our history. I must emphasize that 100% of this Biblical literature is completely consistent with both the Old Testament and the New Testament. There are no contradictions.

Instead, what you are going to read extends the Bible. This book begins eons before the Bible begins. How can this be? It is because Almighty God provided all the accurate information. I am also ensuring complete accuracy that His words and thoughts are published in a very accurate and elegant manner. This entire effort is for every child of God on this planet. God loves each of us so very much it goes beyond our understanding and imagination. If I sound redundant on this point, it is because I purposely am. In no way does this book replace any part of the Bible. It never will and is never intended to do that in any way. This book brings much more detail and extended understanding about the Bible and the life and times of our Lord and Savior Jesus Christ.

God's Astonishing Statement to Me:

I have a personal covenant with our Father to be a fountain of truth in His name on this earth. To publish all that our Father in Heaven wants His children to know about at this time in history. During one of my deep prayerful and meditative sessions with our Father in Heaven, he told me the following words. Yes, these are our Father's exact words. Given to me to publish for all His children. Repeating part of the above:

"My dearest son, Richard," you are the first that I am allowing to speak with me directly and let that be written. You are a unique child of mine and I am very pleased." Almighty God, Your Father

I was completely astonished to hear God say this to me personally. Never did I think or imagine that something like this would happen to me. Yet, it certainly did. As you read through the rest of this book there are many times that Almighty God in The Trinity answered my specific questions. Inspect the content of what is said and get a feel of the authority behind the words. Ask yourself, could a human being make this stuff up. Look at the information that is provided. All of it is consistent with the Bible. The pre-existing covenant with Almighty God is simple. I will always tell His Truth all the time without fail, without omission. Failure to do so will result in the wrath of our Father, whom I love so very much.

You Have a Decision to Make Dear Child of God

You have free will as God has given it to all of us. You are free to choose your reaction to the above statement from Almighty God. This is your choice through free will, either accept this as I have said or reject it now. Your decision will be chronicled in the Akashic records of all mankind.

<u>Now, the decision is yours to believe this or not</u>. Please remember dear sacred child of God, you have a most powerful gift from God that we call free will. Everyone must use their free will even if they do not realize it is a gift from Almighty God. Everyone must use their free will to choose. Is it Almighty God you wish to spend eternity with, or is it Satan in Hell you would rather spend the last part of your existence? As in all things theological and in faith, it is up to you to decide in your heart if this book is something that is from Almighty God or not. It is pretty much that simple.

21

Satan

The Origin of Hate on Earth

Question: But first, my dearest Lord and Savior, while I was resting for a few minutes after writing a lot of the text below, I want to address something that may seem irrelevant but not really. Christians all know about the rebellion of Lucifer within the kingdom. After trying to picture within my mind how the rebellion took place and the subsequent aftermath, it came to me: What did Lucifer look like before his rebellion? What did he look like the moment he was kicked out of the Heavenly Kingdom? In the time frame we use on Earth, how long did his rebellion take place? This is something that I have never ever come across in any Christian literature and it would be wonderful since you were there if you could describe some of these details. If you think this is irrelevant, then thank you for at least listening to this far-out question.

Our Lord and Savior Jesus Christ
April 8, 2025 01:42

Jesus Christ, answer:

Oh, my dearest, dearest of sons, I do love the questions that you bring to me because they illuminate so many facets of all theology and love for the three of us in The Trinity. Lucifer was among the most powerful and beautiful angels of your Heavenly Father. As you know, among other duties, he was responsible for the beautiful and magnificent music within the kingdom, and you will hear that when you arrive. You already know how much your Father loves music.

Now, my answer is far more delicate and complex than you would have thought. You and I have already discussed the other creations of your Heavenly Father. As a scientist, my dear son, you also are very familiar with the concept of equilibrium. You used this a lot during experiments in chemistry in the laboratory. The existence of others of your Heavenly Father's creations does have a minor influence on the creation in which you live. All entities within your Heavenly Father's creations have varying degrees of influence on all the others. Your creation is indeed separate from all others of your father's creations. They have no effect on your lives, and all aspects of existence that you understand exist.

However, there is a minuscule effect your Father's other creation can have on where it is you exist. This is also true for the Heavenly Kingdom and the angelic host. All the angels have a microscopic impact on them that has originated in the other creations. The way to think of this would be that Lucifer was more susceptible to the impact of the other creations. The imperfection within Lucifer, if you want to call it that, is almost imperceptible. However, Lucifer has free will, and the small thought that rose up in the mind of Lucifer could have very easily been ignored, and nothing, and I really do mean nothing, would come of it.

However, through his free will, Lucifer decided to pursue the ungodly path for him, and he started to explore in detail just how beautiful our Heavenly Father made him to be. Out of that, pride and lust were generated within his spirit. Remember, my dearest son, all your Heavenly Father's creations have free will just as you do. Your father's deep love determines he wants all his children to have free will. And it is that which determines the purity of the love his sacred children bestow back upon Him and, of course, the Holy Spirit and me, your Lord and Savior.

So, my dear son, it is NOT a case of some defect in the creation of your Heavenly Father's angels. Your loving, almighty Heavenly Father is pure and perfect in all circumstances across all times. That will never change because remember your Heavenly Father's existence spans across all times. Rather, it brings forth an opportunity to sin against your heavenly Father. But this can only happen if the Angel or the sacred child chooses through their own free will a path that will lead to very bad things happening.

The echoes or consequences of this one decision by Lucifer billions of years ago are still reverberating across the entire creation. These consequences will continue until the End of Times is complete.

Question: My dearest Lord and Savior Jesus Christ,

Most of our Heavenly Father's sacred children on earth believe that Satan has always existed because, within their lives, he always has. But in our previous conversations, I have come to know that it is just not true. My dearest Lord, if you would please describe all existence when it was only our beloved Trinity that existed and without too much detail. Please explain the history of things before the rebellion of Lucifer and anything else after that you would like to tell all our Heavenly Father's sacred children.

Some Thoughts I Wrote Earlier

The origin of hate was long before our Heavenly Father created all His sacred children. Unknown billions of years ago, one of our Heavenly Angels and several other powerful angels decided to rebel against our Father and His throne. It was Lucifer. He fell in love with Himself because he was so beautiful beyond anything he could imagine. Therefore, he felt he was the rightful owner of the throne of existence. Therefore, it was Lucifer who instigated the rebellion and convinced approximately one-third of the angelic hosts to follow Him and also rebel against our loving, Almighty Father.

In an instant this angel named Lucifer was thrown out of the Heavenly kingdom in the blink of an eye along with approximately one third of the angelic host. Simply put, Lucifer became Satan, and the Angels that followed Satan became demons, and over a period, the hatred of Satan and his demons grew worse and worse.

Answer: Our Lord and Savior Jesus Christ:

Oh, my dear son, you certainly do work very hard. You work hard to cover, as you would say, all the bases so that all our Father's sacred children will come to understand why things are the way they are. How things were before Lucifer's rebellion and what is going to happen starting with the End of Times. I congratulate you enormously for all your work for the benefit of all sacred children of our Father. We sincerely, within The Trinity, want to ensure that all necessary knowledge of your Heavenly Father and the history of what has happened will be available to your sacred children. In this way, among others, no one will have any excuse for rejecting your father by saying they just did not know.

Before The Earth Test

I will start at the beginning. Many eons of timeless time ago, there were us three in The Trinity, and there were other creations of your Heavenly Father you will never have access to, which is for your own well-being. Yet to be created is something that would be done only after the three of us in The Trinity agreed to create our sacred children made in our image. It took all three of us to arrive at the physical characteristics and spiritual characteristics of our soon-to-be-born sacred children of our Almighty Father.

As you know my dearest son, we also wanted to match the physical bodies of our children with the environment on Earth. Spiritually speaking, without getting into detail, we wanted to ensure that all our sacred children would have a chance to succeed on Earth. Do they choose to go back to the heavenly kingdom? Or do they choose to reject your Heavenly Father and His rules of life and knowingly sentence themselves into hell where they would ultimately disintegrate through the physical laws of disintegration, as I have said?

Billions of years before this Lucifer and his followers were instantly kicked out of the heavenly kingdom and were banished to earth. And

yes, my dear son, I know you're thinking Satan is present in the rest of the cosmos besides Earth. The answer is yes. The understanding for this answer comes from remembering that the spiritual realm where both all your Father's sacred children reside along with Satan and his demons.

I know you also remember my dearest son that Satan is trans dimensional as your scientists would put it. This is how Satan appeared those three days in front of you trying to scare you but also, he appeared in a different form before Eve in the Garden of Eden. My dear son, The Bible talks mostly about the one appearance of Satan in front of Eve. This is only partially correct. He appeared in front of her multiple times and later he also appeared in front of Adam. They had quite the discussions about whether they should follow the advice of what people call the snake. Everybody knows the outcome of that.

As described in another section of this book, I discuss how I, your author, was attacked directly by Satan and his demons on 3 separate occasions. They are real because, in Satan's attack, his face was no farther away from me than his nose, reaching within 12 inches of my nose.

The details of this horror will be found in another section of this book.

There is nothing in existence that is outside of our Heavenly Holy Trinity.

Said differently, which is our Heavenly Father, His Only Begotten Son Jesus Christ, And Our Blessed Holy Spirit Please remember this

The reason I include the next section in this book is to demonstrate a real-life example of just how powerful and loving Almighty God really is. The next section of this book details just how loving our Almighty Father is. Our loving Father had plans for me to write these books, but my fatal illness threatened to destroy his plans.

If you have a copy of this book in your hands, consider yourself extremely lucky because the earth entered the End of Times in the 1960s. The times ahead for the people on Earth will get harder and harder and more calamitous as time goes on. All of this is outlined in detail in the second book I have published with our Blessed Mother Mary. Its title is "God's **Grand Design, Mother Mary Speaks, Her Apparitions, The End of Times. "One** of the horrifying truths that is described in detail in this second book is the fact that our Pope Francis is indeed the Antichrist. Much proof is provided. **It is undeniable proof that Satan lives in the Vatican.** I got sick to my stomach and depressed several times while writing what our Blessed Mother described as what would happen during the End of Times.

Before we delve into the magnificent stories for you, I should share a few of my personal encounters with the spiritual realm. I have had many spiritual encounters of various kinds, and they ranged from beauty and magnificence on the way to ugly Satanic in nature. You see, my dear reader, Satan knows who I am and where I am always. He does everything he can to destroy me and take me away from my mission in this life. I will only share a few examples that will serve to illustrate the point I believe is essential for you to know about.

Your author gets very angry and yells profanity directly at Satan three times.

Yes, I confess I used a very bad swear word. That was earlier in my life when I was in my 30s. I got very angry at Satan because after we put our two children to bed, I would go back into their room and, in complete amazement at the miracle of my children, was before me. When I was in my children's room, I sat down, and I almost started to cry because I knew they would soon be growing up in a very wicked world. This enraged me to the point that I yelled at Satan directly, and I told Him in no uncertain words, "Go back to Hell where you belong and FU&K you too." If that profanity was not enough, I did yell at him, repeating the 'FU' command three separate times.

Is Satan harmless? NO! Satan relies on lies and half-truths and the gullibility of God's sacred children to induce into a situation something simple. Satan is also very good at converting those sacred children of God that have as their life goal to be very powerful politically or positionally over others of God's sacred children. So many people are attracted to loads of money and other positions of power and influence. It is these people who willingly accept what Satan offers them.

What If Satan Does Appear and yells, Boo!

Do not be afraid of Satan if he decides to knock on your door and go "Boo!" There are some things everyone must know about Satan.

1. He has no real power over any of God's sacred children. **That means you!** He cannot force you to do anything. Although he will try as if that is true. It is not.

2. Satan is extremely clever but is under your "sacred child of God's authority". When Satan or one of his demons appears to me, like many times in one week, he throws nasty words into my mind. Then I say one Hail Mary, one our father, and one Glory Be prayer.

3. **All sacred children of God have authority over Satan,** and after I say those few small prayers, I order Him to leave and go back to hell where he belongs. Every time he had to do what I ordered Him to.

The bottom-line regarding Satan is simply that you can look Him straight in his damned red eyes he's got and tell Him "NO"! In fact, yell at Him NO! Then turn your back and walk away or order Him to go back to hell where he belongs as I do. Now, admittedly, it takes courage to do this, but this is totally within the capabilities of every one of God's sacred children. YES! That means you, too!

Satan appears in our bedroom in the middle of the night.

I did this by doing so within my mind, as all other communications occur within the spiritual realm. So, I got that off my chest, and I thought that was it. Boy, was I wrong. Approximately two or three weeks after my burst of outrage against Satan, in the middle of the night, I heard the loudest crash and bang that I had ever heard. I instantly woke up and looked over to the side of the bed where my wife was still sleeping. Surprisingly, I nudged her and said, "Did you hear that?" She said, "hear what?"

Then, when I turned my head toward the foot of the bed, I got one of the biggest shocks of my life. There he was, Satan Himself, as big as life could be. He looked like Darth Vader but far worse. He was completely black with a cape that went from his left wrist to his right wrist, going over the top of his head like a hood that encapsulated 80% of his head. When I looked at the midsection of his body, it appeared as if I was looking down at an endless tunnel that was the blackest of black. He appeared as if looking at his abdomen area; there was no real substance to his body. There was really something completely ephemeral about his appearance. As I started to gaze upward, I could not help but notice completely that his eyes were a strong glowing red, like a dark shimmering red that was focused completely on your author me.

Satan was approximately seven feet tall. He then bent over the foot of my bed, making his hooded head come within 8 to 10 inches of my nose. It was then, while he was staring directly at my eyes, he started to yell at me. Satan's exact words to me were, **"I will Get You! I will Get You! I Will Get You!" His voice resonated like thunder, and I was wondering instantly whether or not our neighbors could hear it. Was Satan scary? Hell yes! Pardon the pun.**

After he said that he would get me three times, He just stood there over my bed with my wife, and he apparently wanted to maximize the fear factor before he decided to leave. Once he decided to leave, he took his left arm, draped it over his neck area below his chin. Then he looked to his right, and with a flourishing, I heard a whooshing sound, whereupon he then exited our bedroom through the left wall.

This was one of my worst encounters with the spiritual realm. Was this scary? Yes, indeed it certainly was! However, I must point out to everyone that the scare factor of our favorite Satan did not last long. After a while, a minute or two. Well, I realized that if that is all Satan has it's not very much. From other resources, I realized Satan cannot really do physical harm to God's sacred children. He can make things look scary, and he can yell a lot, but that's about it.

The one thing that Satan can do is to tell lies and make the contents of what he says seem ever so appropriate when it is not. For someone like me, Satan has tried to get me to do things only when I am lazy in doing my preparatory prayers to our Lord and Savior Jesus. This opens the door for Satan to attempt to fool me.

Is Satan harmless? NO! It is quite the opposite! Satan relies on lies and half-truths and the gullibility of God's sacred children to induce into a situation something simple. Satan is also very good at converting those sacred children of God that have as their life goal to be very powerful politically or positionally over others of God's sacred children. So many people are attracted to loads of money and other positions of power and influence. It is these people who willingly accept what Satan offers them.

As was mentioned in another place in this book, Satan wanted the Throne of Existence taken away from our loving Almighty Father. Please read slowly and carefully the following words from our Lord and Savior, Jesus Christ.

We already know that Lucifer will rebel against us and through His hatred he will attack our children and tempt all our children to follow Him. <u>We know that most of our children will be fooled and follow Him into hell, where ultimately, they will be dissolved into nothingness</u>. They will go the way of entropy running wild in the physical realm. Those who choose, through their free will and love for us, there create or to love us will join us in an unimaginably beautiful and loving paradise. A paradise where they will live with us forever, eternally, with no end.

This is why there is an Earth and the Earth Test. As Jesus once told me with great love, The Trinity created the physical realm because it provides a place for our Heavenly Father to know His sacred children far better than just the heavenly kingdom. Additionally, the physical earth provides his sacred children a place to live a life reflecting the love of Almighty God. The love within themselves or reject our Heavenly Father and lead a life of sin and therefore send themselves to hell, where they will ultimately disintegrate back into the nothingness from which they came.

It is the Earth test that provides us the decision-making opportunity. We will choose to either live a life of God's laws and rules and go to heaven or reject God's laws of life and in doing so select hell instead. A quick summary is simple: Lead a godly life and spend eternity in the heavenly kingdom or reject God and then go to Hell and disintegrate back into the nothingness from where you came. In other words, you will not exist anymore. There will not even be any memories of you. To others of God's sacred children, it will be as if you never existed.

Hell Is Not Eternal! It Is Worse!

It's shocking but completely true!

One last thought about hell, as I have covered in other parts of my writings: hell is not eternal, and therefore, its citizens are also no longer eternal. Because of the laws of entropy or what our Lord and Savior Jesus Christ calls <u>the law of disintegration</u>; the citizens of Hell will dissolve back into the nothingness from which they came. This means Satan Himself, and it also means all memories of people in hell will also vanish into nothingness as well.

Your author gets very angry and yells a profanity directly at Satan!

Yes, I confess that I used a very bad swear word. Earlier in my life, when I was in 30s. I got very angry at Satan because after we put our two children to bed, I would go back into their room and, in complete amazement at the miracle of my children, was before me. When I was in my children's room, I sat down, and I almost started to cry because I knew they would soon be growing up in a very wicked world. This enraged me to the point that I yelled at Satan directly, and I told Him in no uncertain words, "Go back to Hell where you belong and FU too. If that profanity was not enough, I yelled at him, repeating the 'FU' command three times.

At the time, little did I know that Satan heard what I said. Imagine that! Satan was keeping an eye on me when I did not know it and then I laid an FU bomb on him. He heard what I said, and He was so emotionally incensed that the following event occurred

Satan appears in our bedroom in the middle of the night.

I did this by doing so within my mind, as all other communications occur within the spiritual realm. So, I got that off my chest, and I thought that was it. Boy, was I wrong. Approximately two or three weeks after my burst of outrage against Satan, in the middle of the night, I heard the loudest crash and bang that I had ever heard. I instantly woke up and looked over to the side of the bed where my wife was still sleeping.

Surprisingly, I nudged her and said, "Did you hear that?" She said, "hear what?"

Then, when I turned my head toward the foot of the bed, I got one of the biggest shocks of my life. There he was, Satan Himself, as big as life could be. He looked like Darth Vader but far worse. He was completely black with a cape that went from his left wrist to his right wrist, going over the top of his head like a hood that encapsulated 80% of his head. When I looked at the midsection of his body, it appeared as if I was looking down at an endless tunnel that was the blackest of black. He appeared as if looking at his abdomen area; there was no real substance to his body. There was really something completely ephemeral about his appearance. As I started to gaze upward, I could not help but notice completely that his eyes were a strong glowing red, like a dark shimmering red that was focused completely on your author me.

Satan was approximately seven feet tall. He then bent over the foot of my bed, making his hooded head come within 8 to 10 inches of my nose. It was then, while he was staring directly at my eyes, he started to yell at me. Satan's exact words to me were, **"I will Get You!" "I will Get You!" "I Will Get You!" His voice resonated like thunder, and I was wondering instantly whether or not our neighbors could hear it. Was Satan scary? Hell yes! Pardon the pun.**

After he said that he would get me three times, He just stood there over my bed with my wife, and he apparently wanted to maximize the fear factor before he decided to leave. Once he decided to leave, he took his left arm, draped it over his neck area below his chin, then he looked to his right. And with a flourish, I heard a whooshing sound, whereupon he then exited our bedroom through the left wall.

This was one of my worst encounters with the spiritual realm. Was this scary? Yes, indeed it certainly was! However, I must point out to everyone that the scare factor of our favorite Satan did not last long. After a while, A minute or two Well, I realized that if that is all Satan has it's not very much. From other resources, I realized that Satan cannot really do physical harm to God's sacred children. He can make things look scary, and he can yell a lot, but that's about it.

The one thing that Satan can do is to tell lies and make the contents of what he says seem ever so appropriate when it is not. For someone like me, Satan has tried to get me to do things only when I am lazy in doing my preparatory prayers to our Lord and Savior Jesus. This opens the door for Satan to attempt to fool me.

Is Satan harmless? NO! Satan relies on lies and half-truths and the gullibility of God's sacred children to induce into a situation something simple. Satan is also very good at converting those sacred children of God that have as their life goal to be very powerful politically or positionally over others of God's sacred children. So many people are attracted to loads of money and other positions of power and influence. It is these people who willingly accept what Satan offers them.

What If Satan Does Appear to You and yells, Boo!

Do not be afraid of Satan if he decides to knock on your spiritual door and go "**Boo!**" There are some things everyone must know about Satan.

1. Satan has no real power over any God's sacred children! He always does his best to scare the heck out of God's children and make threats and look as ugly as he can. Remember my dear sacred child, I know precisely what he looks like as described above and I am still here loving our Heavenly Father and The Trinity and our Blessed Mother Mary. Satan cannot harm you by a unilateral action on his part. He cannot force you to do anything you do not want to.

2. He has no real power over any of God's sacred children. **That means you!** Again, He cannot force you to do anything. However, he will try as if He has power over God's sacred children. He does not!

3. Satan is extremely clever but is under your "sacred child of God's authority". When Satan or one of his demons appears to me, like many times in one week, he will throw nasty words into my mind. I say one Hail Mary, one our father, and one Glory Be prayer.

4. **All sacred children of God have authority over Satan,** and after I say those few small prayers, I order Him to leave and go back to

hell where he belongs. Every time he had to do what I ordered Him to.

The bottom-line regarding Satan is simply that you can look Him straight in his damned red eyes he's got and tell Him "NO"! In fact, yell at Him NO! Then turn your back and walk away or order Him to go back to hell where he belongs as I do all the time now. Now, admittedly, it takes courage to do this, but this is totally within the capabilities of every one of God's sacred children. YES! That means you, too!

It's been quite a while since I started this book, and I do not remember if I mention this or not. Because of my naughty big mouth yelling at profanity at Satan I have had to conduct spiritual warfare with not only Satan himself but his evil minions called demons. They know they cannot hurt me as they know they cannot hurt you. But, because now I have become such a juicy target being the anointed messenger our Heavenly Father, I get attacked a lot more than I used to years ago.

Satanic attacks differ in intensity

Depending on the severity of the attack from Satan or one of his lieutenants in his hierarchy, or just a plain demon, I would respond to the attack sometimes by doing nothing. I would simply ignore it. Other times, I will say to whoever is attacking me, "Go back to Hell where you belong!" Beyond that, if the attack were intense, I would say one Our Father and one Hail Mary. Other times, if the attack was louder and more persistent, I would again tell the hellish demon, "Go back to hell where you belong!" Then I would recite one Our Father and one Hail Mary.

One extremely sad example of a satanic figure attacking me is: <u>My Very Own Earthly Father! YES,</u> my dear sacred child of God, you read that last part of the previous sentence correctly. Without getting into any great horrific stories but suffice to say I do not remember once growing up where my father complimented me, or said the three magic words, I love you. On the other side, my father constantly complained about me and kept yelling at me because I was not like him—a lesson to be learned here, dear sacred child of God. Demons want your behavior to become more and more like theirs while they are on earth.

Long before my father died, I knew he was going to hell. How did I know that? I will sum things up by simply saying: God is the perfection of the deepest of love. My father was just the opposite — an extremely hateful and cruel man, especially towards me. I was the only helpless target for him because I was an only child. He was the kind of man who would take away a little boy's love of his life, meaning his dog. Yes, my dear sacred children, my father took away my dog from me because he lied and said, "My dog made me sneeze too much." After only a few weeks of enjoying" Cubby", my dad announced that the dog is returning to the pound. He knew that would hurt me greatly.

After he died, while I was in my meditation room, he would come up through the floor looking not like himself, but the image of excrement. Yes, the previous sentence is a valid objective observation. I tell you this only because it is entirely accurate, and this is what happens to mean and cruel people. He appeared either 4 or 5 times, I am not sure. After I told him, "Go back to hell, and stay there!" I added the extra three words, "and stay there"; he never came up from the floor again.

Remember, dear sacred child of God, you have control over those hellish demons, which, again, means Satan himself. Also, words mean a lot in the spiritual realm. The addition of those three words prevented my father from ever spending the enormous amount of energy he needed to rise to where he was visible to me.

22

God's Sacred Children's Exposure To Satan and The Earth Test

Dear Lord: When was Lucifer's rebellion? Was it before or after God created all His sacred children? I believe it had to be before our Father loved us into existence.

Think about this through, dear son. Your Father knew long before we decided to create children in His image that Lucifer, one of His mighty angels, would rebel against Him in a horrifically sinful manner. Under no circumstances would God allow His sacred children to be exposed to Lucifer's evil while you were in the Heavenly Kingdom. This means that before you were lovingly created in your Father's image, Lucifer and His followers were cast out of the Heavenly Kingdom. Also, he was cast out long before the earth had developed to the point where it would support human life.

Potential Sacred Children Sin:

So, at some point in the vast history of your sacred existence, simultaneously, the conditions were that you were not created yet. Lucifer and His rebel angels had been cast out of the Heavenly realm down to the pre-existing Spiritual realm, the part called hell made special for

His demons, and to the earth where Lucifer, now called Satan, was forced to dwell with His angels, now called demons. Only after this did all of us in The Trinity engage in the glorious and loving creation of each special and unique one of God's sacred children. You were then great citizens of the Heavenly realm where there was no conflict, where there was no Lucifer or rebellious angels.

No sin in the air would tempt any of God's children. This is why every one of you was utterly sinless and was unable to succumb to temptation of any kind. All that potential sin was previously cast out of the Heavenly Kingdom when Lucifer and His angels were gone.

Now, after that, because of Lucifer's pride bubbled up from deep inside Him, it became unavoidable that you, in some manner in infinite time, would be exposed to sin within the multiple creations of Almighty God.

You may ask how an angel created in perfection could have such a negative emotion deep inside them. I will not go into all the details, but I will tell you that it has to do with the balance of all creations and the symmetry of everything in its totality. Remember, all God's children have no knowledge of everything else that occurs in created form from your Heavenly Father. There is the "other" that exists as well. That is all I want to tell you currently.

All of this is the background to answer your first question: you were given a choice to come to the earth to be tested by your free will to choose your eternal destiny. Choose God for eternal paradise, live with The Trinity in the Heavenly Kingdom, and voluntarily obey the rules set forth for His children. Or choose to succumb to Satan's lure of false freedom and slowly dissolve back into nothingness from where everything associated with Satan will go.

Were all of God's children given a free choice of whether to be born on the earth? Yes! God will never force Himself upon anything within all His creations. All have a choice. You, my dearest son, made your choice to live on the earth for a blink in time to resolve your eternal destiny. As I told you before, my dearest one, before you were born, you chose to live a life where you will always put others ahead of yourself. This is a remarkable choice while you were still within the Heavenly Kingdom. You wanted to emulate what is the essence of The Trinity. And so, you have lived such a life, and you are yet to know and feel the glorious amount of love that is waiting for you when you return. You have suffered so much in the name of your Almighty Father.

All these choices are also available to every one of your Father's unique children. As it turns out, almost all of God's Spiritual children chose to live a life on earth. They wanted to be tested on their love for their Father and His ways. In this manner, everything deep inside each child will be exposed for all to see, including themselves. Many times, even God's sacred children do not know or are aware of what lurks at the core of their free will. In a sense, you could call this a purification process for the benefit of all God's children and the physical and Spiritual realms. <u>All of God's sacred children did know that if they had fatal free will flaws deep inside them, living within the Heavenly Kingdom would be torturous for them. This is because living a Holy life would seem like a prison to them sooner or later. They would rather know now by going to earth and finding out what boils inside them.</u>

Note: The Unbounded Love of Jesus at My Request for Someone in Hell:

A long time ago, I knew a woman who was very lovely, and she attended church with me. However, after a few months, I knew her well enough that she was horrifically abused by her mother. So, too, was her sister. Her sister turned out to be an alcoholic. She had to attend alcohol anonymous. The lady I knew eventually could not hide the rage-filled person she was. No one can hide from horrific abuse from one or the other parent. Her childhood was identical to mine, except it was my father who abused me. For her, it was her mother.

About three months later, we went our separate ways. One day much later, I asked our Lord and Savior, Jesus Christ, how she was doing. *He said,", my dear son, it is sad to say that your friend committed suicide." Because of that and other sins, she is now in hell. Her life while growing up was almost identical to yours.* I have felt strongly that she and I suffered from identical childhoods. Except in her case, she was unable to overcome the horrific childhood cruelty she had like mine.

I felt that she was a victim of cruel violence, just like me. I asked Jesus, as a personal favor to me, if He would please give her a second chance at entering Heaven. I knew of the horrors and mental torment she went through her whole life because of very powerful parental abuse. Jesus said yes. This meant that she would have to again go through Heavenly counseling and be exposed to the manner of behavior within the Heavenly Kingdom. This is the immense love that Jesus has for every one of us. The terrible sadness of this story is underlined in the previous paragraph.

She was psychologically damaged so severely that she could not escape the awful damage to her inner psyche. Later, she asked Jesus to go back to hell. Knowing she would ultimately be dissolved back into nothingness because she could not in any way adhere to the necessary behavioral requirements for life in the Heavenly Kingdom.

I left out parts of this story when, after she died, she contacted me when she was crying her eyes out and in the middle of being tortured by a few of Satan's demons. I will never forget the crying, the shrieking, and pleading with me to help her. I will not tell you anything more as it still brings awful tears to my eyes and loving heart.

Please take heed of this real-life story. I can only imagine how countless times things like this have happened to many of our Heavenly Father's sacred children, yet everything is subject to the free will of all His sacred children.

Our Powerful Free Will

Free will is an overwhelmingly powerful gift to give to everyone. God did not want to create drones or robots. All of us in The Trinity wanted those children who love us with their own choice of free will. What pleasure is derived from being loved only because they were told to? That kind of love is an imposter and not love at all. This would fly into the face of the true character of the three of us in The Trinity. As I said, I am the way, the truth, and life on earth. It is the truth that everything works in such a loving manner. Without that, nothing is worth anything at all. It is the truth of each child's free will that guides their destiny one way or the other.

Now, what about the few of God's sacred children who were afraid to look inside themselves and go to earth to find out? Consistent with our deep love for all our children, they may stay inside the Heavenly Kingdom for all eternity. However, they will live freely in a restricted part of the Kingdom. Their lives will be utterly glorious. They will be filled with the love of us in The Trinity. And the love of the angels that surround them and serve them, and all the other children who preferred to stay in the Kingdom and not sojourn to earth. Their existence will indeed be joyous and excellent for all eternity. But they will do so in a much smaller and restricted part of the Heavenly Kingdom. All of us love them so very much that they will be ever so happy and do the things that they enjoy, whatever that may be.

My dear son, I hope that this answers your simple question. The answer, however, is complex yet simple at the same time. I hope I have given you an understandable context in which all of this occurs. I love you."

Yes! You certainly answered my question and gave all of us children much more beautiful information about the context in which this occurs. We all benefit from knowing so much more about our existence and how God's creations work together.

Secrets, They Are Impossible

There are no secrets within the Spiritual realm, nor should there ever be, for our Father is not like that in any way. Said differently, our Father in Heaven is not limited in any way throughout all His creations. Like St. John said in His gospel, "No matter where I go, dear Father, you are always there. "

Remember that our Holy Father, when we were loved into existence, loved each of us so much that He left a part of Himself within our Spiritual being. It is in this way that our prayers will be heard by our Heavenly Father with no exceptions. You may feel that God did not hear what your prayer request was or something of that nature; your Heavenly Father did indeed hear every word that you said to Him.

Before you finish your prayer, please remember to ask our Heavenly Father to respond to you so that you know it is Him. With the information or request that you have prayed for, it is essential that you do this because that way, you will be listening to the response of our Heavenly Father. All prayers are answered in one way or another. To each sacred child of our Father, pay close attention to when our Father responds to you. Our Father also knows every thought we have, all our feelings, our emotions, and our intentions. Everything we think and experience. There are NO secrets from God, NONE! All three members of our sacred Holy Trinity are ever so close to each of us that it is hard to imagine just how close they really are.

It is impossible for within all the cosmos or any other part of creation to contain any kind of secret anywhere at all. Everything is just transparent. This comes as a big surprise for all the crooks on earth when they die and have their life reviewed with Jesus. Please remember that in our Blessed Holy Bible, there is a verse in the New Testament where Jesus says:

<u>"I Am the Way and The Truth and The Life.</u>

<u>No One Comes to The Father Except Through Me."</u> <u>John 14: 6</u>

A Note After Our Creation

You and I are the sacred Spiritual children of Almighty God, our Holy Father, who loves every one of us. After our Father created all His children, for an undetermined length of time, all of us would stay with The Trinity in the Heavenly Kingdom. Here, we children would be nurtured and loved, explore the Heavenly realm, and play with our Almighty Father in so many ways. We also learned about the values given by our Father. This includes all His characteristics and personality and His unlimited love.

This gave our Father such infinite joy and happiness to be with His children. Additionally, this time for us within the Kingdom of Heaven before we were born into the physical earth. This gave us time to learn about our Almighty Father, His creation, about ourselves and mature in the direction of the talents and personal characteristics that our Father intended for each of us. Remember, each child is individually unique. No two are the same.

We learned about ourselves and all creation inside the Heavenly realm and outside it as well. We played games with our loving Father. He nurtured us and told us wonderful stories about the creation to come. It was a wonderland of delight, full of joy, happiness, and fulfillment, especially when our Father would teach us about so many delightful things that are yet to come. Our Father's sacred children were happy beyond human description when we would play with Him and enjoy with all the other children in the Heavenly Kingdom. All of us matured in different ways, none the same, all different as was and is the will of our Father.

Over what we now call time; each sacred child was created unique and different from every other child. Therefore, each child grew in various ways from all the others. Each one of us was becoming more of a unique, one-of-a-kind individual child of God. God does not ever use a cookie-cutter in any of His creations, no matter what it may be.

<u>The reason for all creation is a monumental act of love for God's sacred children. It is to use this pathway back to the origin of our existence in the Heavenly Kingdom and life with our Heavenly Father for all eternity.</u>

23

God's Sacred Children: A Choice About the Earth Test or Not

We were all aware that we would be given a choice to choose if we wanted to come to earth or not. Nothing is ever forced on us. Father never forces anything upon us because he gave us our own individual free will. It is here on the earth that we would live for a short time to choose which path we would take. Before we were born into the physical, we had to pass through the process of forgetting and many other preparations that included what our life on earth would be like. Our knowledge of Heaven we could not take with us to earth all that we were taught and experienced in the Heavenly realm. That is known as "the forgetting." For those who return to Heaven, their complete knowledge will return. That would stay behind us until we returned to our Father in Heaven. To make a pure choice of what we wanted our destiny to be, we had to leave behind the experiences and knowledge we gained in Heaven.

Each child's choice is demonstrated for all eternity by how we conduct our Spiritual and physical lives on the earth. Each child demonstrates their choice by living according to God's laws and love for each other…or not! All creation watches and observes our behavior and how we choose. There are no hidden secrets within all of God's creation. This is so when some children think they can hide something. All criminals believe this is true, that they

can hide things. They are wrong. It is impossible by God's design to keep hidden anything within His creation.

God's children would need to make this choice during their lives on earth, where Satan has access to them because remember that the physical realm and the Spiritual overlap each other. Also, remember that all of God's sacred children are part Spiritual and part physical. Our Spiritual part gives God's children direct access to their Father in Heaven. Satan has access to our minds, which is Spiritual.

Individually, God's sacred children would be born into this Spiritual and physical realm using the human bodies their Father and the rest of The Trinity had designed for us to occupy with our Spiritual being. Our bodies on earth were designed by God to perfectly match the Spiritual and physical realms that their loving Father created for us. It was this combination of the two realms with the two parts of the human body. Our minds and Spirit allowed God's children to communicate with their Father in Heaven. Our physical bodies made it possible to experience the trials and tribulations that come with the physical realm. It also provides for us to procreate children so that they, too, can live a physical life on earth.

We know the risks of life on earth with no guarantee that we will make it back to the Heavenly Kingdom. The whole purpose of going to Earth is to take the Earth test, and in its simplest terms, it will reveal the depths of our inner selves as Spiritual beings. Specifically, it will demonstrate whether we will go to Heaven or to hell. We demonstrate how we live our lives and how closely we follow the rules of life for us children while on earth. That is what this book is all about: knowing what we need to do to return to Heaven.

Knowing what I just shared, 90% of your Father's sacred children in Heaven will decide to come to Earth for the Earth test. The remaining 10% will stay in Heaven and live magnificent lives, although more restricted than those who pass the Earth test and return to the Heavenly Kingdom. God loves them just as much as everyone else. They are not second-class citizens.

Unknown to us children, their first two parents on this earth, called Adam and Eve, had made a grave error by disobeying our Almighty Father. Against God's explicit instructions, they ate from the tree of the knowledge of good and evil. They gave in to the lies of Satan posing as a snake. This permanently stained our first two parents with sin and then all their human descendants that would be born on planet Earth. And so, this is the heritage of all human beings on planet Earth.

There Are Only Two Foundational / Moral and Ethical Forces in All of Creation

1. The <u>Infinite Love</u> of Almighty God
2. The <u>Horrific Hatred</u> That Comes from Satan himself and his demons

Nobody thinks about this, but being our Heavenly Father's Anointed Messenger, it's appropriate within my prayers and meditations these subjects are extremely important for all His sacred children to be aware, understand and adhere to.

Life comes at us on Earth as a blizzard of this, that, and the other thing. Our minds get preoccupied by many different things every day of our life, and it is hard to sort out what is what and how to be a loving and good Christian.

I believe this will surprise almost everyone. But yes…

<u>There are so many different manifestations to describe the love of Almighty God and how it holds all of creation together. In fact, it is Godly love that keeps all of creation together.</u>

<u>Those forces are simply Godly love as number one. The second force is Satanic hatred.</u> There is not a third. Hate comes in different forms like dishonesty, keeping secrets, fighting the good forces on Earth, violating the Ten Commandments, and violations of the three laws of existence, all of which come from our Heavenly Father.

We all are here on Earth to take the <u>Earth Test,</u> which is simply do we decide to love as our Heavenly Father does or do, we lead sinful lives that are promoted by Satan. How we live our lives creates a testimony to which of the two we have chosen: is it love from our Almighty Father, or is it hate from Satan? The way we lead our lives is the testimony to which choice our inner spiritual choice is. Is it Almighty God, or is it Satan?

Our Heavenly Father has always existed throughout all eternity. There never was a time when our Almighty Father did not exist. Our Heavenly Father is the alpha and the Omega. Always was and always will be. Our Heavenly Father brings together the other two members of The Trinity. The second member is our Lord and Savior, Jesus Christ. He is the only begotten son of our Heavenly Father and is seated at the right hand of the Father for all eternity. The third member is our sacred Holy Spirit. Our Holy Spirit plays a vital role in ensuring that there is continuity that exists and always will exist within creation.

Note: I will be writing a book later this year that will concentrate on the role that our Holy Spirit plays in bringing all the pieces of creation together.

The Origin of Love on Earth

Through all of infinity, love always existed. There was never a time in which love did not exist throughout all the dimensions of this creation. For that matter, this love also includes all the other creations of our Heavenly Father to which we have no knowledge and no access. But it's very simple to see and understand even these other dimensions and creations are based on the same characteristics our Heavenly Father brings forth to us in this creation that we live in.

We call our creation the universe which is an inaccurate term. It is the term that is used for only the manifestation of the physical realm. The spiritual realm is where the unseen part of each of us resides. Our physical bodies are where our individual spiritual selves occupy for our lifetime. So, there was no origin of love because our Heavenly Father and The Trinity have always existed throughout all infinite timelines.

When the creation we live in, the spiritual realm, the physical is magnificently and purposely designed to accommodate our physical bodies, they were all created within an atmosphere of pure love that has no boundaries. When each of us was created unique from all the rest, we were created in a completely loving environment. We were created within the Heavenly Kingdom, and sin never existed, nor will it ever exist within our Father's kingdom. After each of us was created, all of us had absolutely no concept of what sin was.

However, many eons before all the angels were created, our Heavenly Father already knew that one of his angels would rebel against him. This is the first wretched sin that existed ever so long ago. In no way is sin tolerated. Lucifer, as mentioned before, was the Angel who basically fell in love with himself. And because of his beauty, he felt he was more deserving of the Kingly throne in the kingdom and tried to overthrow our Heavenly Father. I do not know how long Lucifer survived in the kingdom before he was thrown out, along with approximately one-third of the angelic host. But the amount of time was far less than what we would call a second. Lucifer and his demonic host were thrown out of the Heavenly Kingdom in the blink of an eye and were thrown down to Earth, where we now live.

The Origin of Hate on Earth

The origin of hate was long before our Heavenly Father created all His sacred children. Unknown billions of years ago, one of our Heavenly Angels and several other powerful angels decided to rebel against our Father and His throne. It was Lucifer, keeper of all the divine kingdom music. During the work he did, it came to him that he was so beautiful he was more deserving of our Father's throne than our Almighty Father. He fell in love with himself because he was so beautiful beyond anything he could imagine. Therefore, he felt he was the rightful owner of the throne of existence. Therefore, it was Lucifer who instigated the rebellion and convinced approximately one-third of the angelic hosts to follow Him and also rebel against our loving, Almighty Father.

In an instant this angel named Lucifer was thrown out of the Heavenly Kingdom in the blink of an eye along with approximately one third of the angelic host. Simply put, Lucifer became Satan, and the Angels that followed Satan became demons, and over a period, the hatred of Satan and his demons grew worse and worse. As is described in another section of this book, I discuss how I, your author, was attacked directly by Satan and his demons on 3 separate occasions. They are real because, in Satan's attack, his face was no farther away from me than his nose, reaching within 12 inches of my nose.

There is nothing in existence that is outside of our Heavenly Holy Trinity.

Said differently, which is our Heavenly Father, His Only Begotten Son Jesus Christ, And Our Blessed Holy Spirit Please remember this

The reason I include the next section in this book is to demonstrate a real-life example of just how powerful and loving Almighty God really is. The next section of this book details just how loving our Almighty Father is. Our loving Father had plans for me to write these books, but my fatal illness threatened to destroy his plans. So, He healed me.

24

The Beginning of The End Times

President Lyndon Baines Johnson started the Vietnam War

Remember this, America! Our great country was a beautiful place to live in after World War II up until the 1960s when the End of Times began with Democrat President Lyndon Baines Johnson's Great Society. Then things turned into one damned political lie after another. Our country still has not recovered from WWII. Politics in our country is now Satanic up one side and down the other. Johnson's "Great Society" was a colossal lie. Within this satanic federal assistance bill, President Johnson, to get government financial assistance, the husband had to move out of his own home, leaving his family behind. It did not take a genius to figure out that the Great Society was completely Satanic in its foundations.

This was completely Satanic, with the intention of breaking up families as much as they could. Remember that families reflect the will and image of Almighty God. Only a Satanically driven person would purposely break up sacred families. This is what Johnson did. Remember, my dear sacred children, it is God's intention that a woman and a man be married in holy matrimony to lovingly produce the next generation of God's sacred children. Even back then, the Democrat Party was Satanic because the will of our Heavenly Father was to have both man and woman together raising their children. Lyndon Johnson purposely and willfully destroyed that for what he thought would be a political advantage for the Democrat Party. On a flight on Air Force One, it has been reported by observers that President Johnson said, "I will have them nig*ers voting Democrat for the next 200 years."

I also remember Democrat Lyndon Baines Johnson starting the Vietnam War, where he sent many thousands of our soldiers to die in the jungles. He started that war with the excuse that North Vietnam attacked one of our Navy destroyers in the Gulf of Tonkin. He lied to our country. **That**

attack never happened, as was revealed years later. The result was that 58,000 US military personnel died before we lost the war and pulled out. Add to that the more significant number of wounded soldiers and those who were mentally destroyed for the rest of their lives.

I was an army ROTC Cadet being groomed to become an officer in the Army during the beginning of the Vietnam War that President Johnson created. However, in my case, I had lifelong asthma and migraine headaches that disqualified me from military service. So, instead of going to Vietnam and killing people, I went to graduate school in business.

Enslaving The Black Community to Federal Government Handouts

As said before, but it bears repeating for poor people, which were almost all people, including black people at the time to get government help, the father and family head had to leave his home. This purposely destroyed untold hundreds of thousands, if not millions, of black families. Families where the children didn't get the benefit of a father who would teach them discipline, manners, respect, dealing with life outside the home, and many other good examples for children when they grow up.

So many black kids and others being fatherless grew up having no direction in their lives, no sense of wanting to accomplish something, and so on. The mother of the house was utterly overwhelmed, just trying to work for enough money to pay the rent and put food and clothing on their children. Her work plus government money made feeding her children and paying for household expenses barely possible. What President Johnson did supported by the Democrat Party, destroyed the social fabric. Know that love is a very important part of our country's communities and social construction.

Being a practicing Christian back then was a highly regarded and honorable thing to be. It was not a status symbol but rather a sign of a healthy family. Now, in 2025, Christians are attacked from all sides. Recently, 700 churches have been destroyed or closed in our country. Like it or not, this is a prime example of the trend that President Satanic Baines Johnson established so many years ago. The amount of anger that built up within our communities and social structure grew and grew. Along the way, the Democrat Party fueled the hatred against Almighty God, as was exemplified by the Catholic Church.

Enough on this remember always that Democrat Lyndon Baines Johnson kicked off the End of Times as described by our Blessed Mother Mary in her new book titled.

*"**God's Grand Design, Blessed Mother Mary Directly Speaks,***

Her Apparitions and The End of Times"

Life today in 2025

Today, our government has grown every year from the 1950s to 2025. That is 74 years. Democrat President Joe Biden wants to increase the IRS by 80,000 new agents to collect more and more and more taxes from our shrinking middle class of hardworking people. Being gifted with some spiritual gifts, I know that his goal is to make as many people as possible dependent on government benefits. This moves the citizens of our country closer and closer to living in a communist society. Our government and we citizens of America are also becoming more and more Satanic in our behavior. Now, sinful behavior seems to permeate the air wherever you turn.

One measure of a Satan-filled political party is what the Democrats did during their national convention. During the Democrat Convention yesterday, they bragged about instituting mobile vans that would provide free vasectomies and <u>free abortions</u> to anybody who wanted them, no questions asked. This is a new low in our country's morals and ethics and basically giving the finger to our loving Almighty God. Hay! There is the truck; let's get the abortion.

Our schools have been taken over by Satanic powers. Instead of teaching reading, writing, and arithmetic as when I was a child, they spend so much time indoctrinating our gullible children with Satanic propaganda our children cannot even define what a woman is. In some cases, a woman can change from day to day, depending on how she feels. Small children are given sex education and told anything goes. Our very young children are being educated on how to suck a man's penis. Yea! That is painfully true.

25

The Scientific Side of What Objective Reality Is

A few scientific answers to our beloved three-word question.

No one on earth has ever devised an all-inclusive definition of what life is. Every definition I have ever run across is basically secular and scientific in nature and falls far short of what life really is. In other words, all definitions are fundamentally physical in nature with a hodgepodge of so-called scientific jargon. Each explanation of what life is completely ignores the true source of all life, which is Almighty God. As I have indicated multiple times throughout this book, human beings are really two separate beings combined into one.

Our eternal part of us is purely spiritual in nature and will live for all eternity unless we reject our Heavenly Father and go to hell. The other half of us is the physical part. It is this part that allows us to live on Earth and take the Earth test. It is this test that we declare to all of creation our decision on where we want to spend eternity. Our decision is clearly displayed in the way we live our lives. Do we live our lives according to the three Godly rules of life and the 10 Commandments as described earlier?

Or do we choose to ignore God's rules of existence and instead follow the sinful temptations of Satan? In that case, we are condemning ourselves to hell. I should point out that God never sends anyone to hell. We send ourselves to Hell! Once we realize the destructiveness that we have caused during our lifetime. It is then that each of the people who are destined for hell will understand completely why there is no place for them in the Heavenly Kingdom.

What is Life? General Characteristics of Life, The Secular Scientific Versions

The scientific physical side of things. Life is a living matter, and, as such, it exhibits certain attributes that include responsiveness, growth, metabolism, energy, transformation, and reproduction. From my physiological perspective, life is defined as any system capable of performing functions such as eating, metabolizing, excreting, breathing, moving, growing, reproducing, and responding to external stimuli.

These definitions of life could go on and on. If you ask a scientist what life is, you will receive a definition that stems directly from their scientific specialty. Anything a scientist says is confined to the physical and secular version and does not even come close to what life truly is.

Our beloved Bible has the answer regarding what life is. The answer can be found in Genesis, but it is then expanded upon in other parts of the Bible, including both the Old Testament and the New Testament, across its 66 unique books. Keeping things remarkably simple, human life on Earth has two inescapable aspects: a physical body, which is what all scientists limit themselves to, and our Spiritual body, which no scientist could ever understand. I have degrees in Chemistry and Physics. One of our axioms was that if you cannot measure it, it does not exist. Graduate degrees include a business degree and, later in life, a master's degree in Pastoral Ministry with a specialty in Spirituality.

My academic training, therefore, covers both the Spiritual realm and the physical realm in detail. Human life is the marriage of both the physical bodies we inhabit for a short time and our Spiritual bodies, which are the essence of who and what we are. The Spiritual bodies are eternal beings created by our Heavenly Father. Remember this above all else. When our physical bodies pass away, it is our Spiritual bodies that will continue onward, living for all eternity with our loving Almighty Father. Unfortunately, those of us who do not live our lives according to our Father's laws of Life will not join the rest of us when we go back to the Heavenly Kingdom.

It is true the members of The Trinity and our Blessed Mother feel great remorse for all those sacred children of Almighty God. The sacred children that have not lived their lives in a Godly manner and, therefore, will not be citizens of the Heavenly Kingdom. They will instead be relegated to hell, where their natural entropy will rapidly increase to a point where no order remains to maintain a coherent body. Our Lord and Savior calls this the law of disintegration. Everyone will disintegrate back into the random nothingness from which God created them.

Scientifically, what is the ultimate origin of our Earthly life? (Polluted with politics)

We know that we are not a pile of accidental chemicals that, over time, bumping into each other somehow formed our physical bodies. That is complete and utter nonsense. There is no secular explanation of where our bodies come from, and certainly NOT where our spiritual bodies come from either. Does anyone think that Charles Darwin had the Magic Formula many decades ago for where our bodies come from? If anybody believes that, they are sadly mistaken. I bet many of them do not realize that if they believe that hogwash Darwinian interpretation, they also are automatically denying the existence of Almighty God and denying the very source of their own existence.

It is incredible that some people are so ignorant and gullible they believe a botanist who worked for a few months in the Galapagos Islands produced a theory that explains everything. It explains that all human life is just beyond anything that has the slightest tendency of intelligence to it. Now, I am not a Darwin hater by any means. In fact, I consider him to be a very good scientist and botanist. In his book The Origin of Species, he said <u>it is shown that the changes in a species over time cannot be explained by a sequence of many minor changes. Then my theory is wrong.</u> I recommend his book to anybody, frankly. I would enjoy immensely having a deep discussion with Charles Darwin as I do respect him very much for his work. Unfortunately, politicians and those who want to make a profit from misinterpreting his books, mutilating the meanings of what he is in his scientific work. The Democrat Party today is guilty of gargantuan lies about what he said and what he meant in his corpus of scientific endeavors.

Author's personal note: I have been exposed to Darwinian theory for the last 50 or 60 years. As you may have encountered, the documentation of my scientific training does include chemistry, both organic and inorganic, some nuclear and quantitative, along with a full year of biochemistry and biology itself. I won't mention all my credentials, but I was also employed as a research scientist at NASA for upper atmospheric quantitative and qualitative particulate analysis, utilizing sophisticated electron microscopes. I am qualified to evaluate the scientific method as it may or may not be applied in different situations.

I feel I am qualified to say the following. Our highly esteemed Charles Darwin was an excellent botanist. His reports certainly indicate that. That is the proper term for what he was engaging in. He did excellent work on the birds that existed in the Galapagos Islands and characterized them quite well. However, long after Dr Darwin's life came to an end, politicians got hold of his work. Warning: One Rule of Life is: If you want to screw something up, tangle it terribly, and waste a lot of money doing it, give it to a politician. Our Democrat Party in the United States is by far the most dishonest and wretched organization that I have ever encountered in my almost 80 years on the planet. I have never seen such horrific lies spew out of these politicians' mouths. Do not believe what politicians tell you regarding Charles Darwin, the Galapagos Islands, and the resulting small, very small changes in the size of native bird beaks over a relatively long period of time. That is what Charles Darwin was measuring, and it has absolutely nothing to do with any other organisms, especially mammals like you and me.

Author's note:

I should tell you as well that my amazing and loving Lord Jesus Christ, has been counseling me for the last 4 or 5 months. Counseling regarding the need for me and my family to move out of the area that we currently live in. There will be many violent earthquakes in California especially up and down the San Francisco Peninsula. These earthquakes are not fooling around. They will be far stronger than what has happened in the past. Food shortages will appear rapidly along with electricity and water. We live in the San Jose area, and it is just sitting there prime to be destroyed by an earthquake similar in size to the 1905 earthquake. Also, given the horrific crime rate in our country, where we live in San Jose CA will be horrifically impacted by crime and other sorts of person to personal thievery and so on.

Like all congested parts of our country, where we live will be in the process of disintegration into chaos and other forces that will destroy our country and our culture. So, I told this to my entire family. And most of us will be moving toward the Lake Tahoe area but not too high up for snow. It is a safe area to live and crime rates are next to zero. Take heed, my dearest readers; move out of natural disaster areas and move especially away from congested areas in cities and go far more rural areas that are still.

Science

No one on earth has ever devised an all-inclusive definition of what life is. Every definition I have ever encountered is essentially secular and scientific in nature, falling far short of what life truly is. All definitions are fundamentally physical in nature, with a hodgepodge of so-called scientific jargon. Each explanation of what life is completely ignores the true source of all life, which is Almighty God.

Our magnificent revelation of how life begins in all its forms will bring great satisfaction and love to your heart. And if you are like me, tears of joy and happiness will well up in your eyes. It is far more than you currently know, so stay tuned for what I'm about to say. It will warm your heart and, frankly, give you a magnificent sense of belonging to the Heavenly Kingdom.

As I have indicated multiple times throughout this book, human beings are really two separate beings combined into one.

Our eternal part of us is purely spiritual in nature and will live for all eternity unless we reject our Heavenly Father and go to hell. The other half of us is the physical part. It is this part that allows us to live on Earth and take the Earth test. It is this test that we declare to all of creation our decision on where we want to spend eternity. Our decision is clearly displayed in the way we live our lives. Do we live our lives according to the three Godly rules of life and the 10 Commandments as described earlier?

Or do we choose to ignore God's rules of existence and instead follow the sinful temptations of Satan? In that case, we are condemning ourselves to hell. I should point out that God never sends anyone to hell. We send ourselves to Hell! Once we realize the destructiveness that we have caused during our lifetime. Then, each of the people destined for hell will understand completely why there is no place for them in the Heavenly kingdom.

What is Life? The Godless Versions

The scientific and physical side of things. Life is a living matter, and, as such, it exhibits certain attributes that include responsiveness, growth, metabolism, energy, transformation, and reproduction. From my physiological perspective, life is defined as any system capable of performing functions such as eating, metabolizing, excreting, breathing, moving, growing, reproducing, and responding to external stimuli.

These definitions of life could go on and on. If you ask a scientist what life is, you will receive a definition that stems directly from their scientific specialty. Anything a scientist says is confined to the physical and secular version and does not even come close to what life truly is.

Our beloved Bible has the answer regarding what life is. The answer can be found in Genesis, but it is then expanded upon in other parts of the Bible, including both the Old Testament and the New Testament, across its 66 unique books. Keeping things remarkably simple, human life on Earth has two inescapable aspects: a physical body, which is what all scientists limit themselves to, and our Spiritual body, which no scientist could ever understand. I have degrees in Chemistry and Physics. One of our axioms was that if you cannot measure it, it does not exist. Graduate degrees include a business degree and, later in life, a master's degree in Pastoral Ministry with a specialty in Spirituality.

My academic training, therefore, covers both the Spiritual realm and the physical realm in detail. Human life is the marriage of both our physical bodies and our Spiritual bodies, which are actually the essence of who and what we are, which are eternal beings created by our Heavenly Father. Remember this above all else. When our physical bodies pass away, it is our Spiritual bodies that will continue onward, living for all eternity with our loving Almighty Father. Unfortunately, those of us who choose not to live our lives according to our Father's laws of life will not join the rest of us when we return to the Heavenly Kingdom.

It is true the members of The Trinity and our Blessed Mother do indeed feel remorse for all those sacred children of Almighty God who have not lived their lives in a Godly manner. Therefore, they will not be citizens of the Heavenly Kingdom. They will instead be relegated to hell, where their natural entropy will rapidly increase to a point where no order remains to maintain a coherent body. Our Lord and Savior calls this the law of disintegration. Everyone will disintegrate back into the random nothingness from which God created them.

Satan Has Infiltrated Our Government at All Levels

I have never seen so much Satanic infiltration across the entire world as I have seen over the last 30 years or so. This is especially true for the United States of America. It used to be that small children could walk down the street without fearing something terrible happening to them. Now, one of their parents must be with them all the time to protect them from the enormous number of criminals in our country. I think I said this before, but in elementary school, I could walk to school without the slightest fear of anything bad happening. Not so anymore. Now, small children can be snatched off the street and sold in the sex market and worse.

All things rotten have increased dramatically since the Biden administration, along with Kamala Harris, started to run our federal government. Our southern border does not exist anymore because of the direct and purposeful actions of our President Biden. There were 94 executive orders from Pres. Trump that made sure the southern border is strong. Within a few days of being elected, our southern border was entirely opened by dismissing every good thing Pres. Trump has done for our citizens. Our country, as of now, when this is written, has spent more than 88 billion dollars on illegal aliens. When it comes to providing housing for illegals, the government has seized a lot of first-class hotels while kicking out our military veterans onto the street. If you do not believe this, please look it up at an objective source of information.

My next book will address all the horrific crimes that have been allowed into our country, but also all the crimes that have been directly committed by the Democrat party. I have stated in my previous book, co-authored by our Blessed Mother Mary, the following sentence:

The Democrat Party Is the Political Arm of Satan. This Is All Part Of The End of Times and Has Been Specifically and In Detail Described By Our Blessed Mother Mary. [20]

I have never seen so many lies coming from all levels of government. Their policies are horrifically destructive to our way of life. This includes local school boards, where they allow pornography in elementary school libraries, and they feel that parents have no say in their children's education. These people are tyrannical and driven by Satan himself.

There have been monstrous changes within our country since the 1950s when I was a child growing up in Chicago. With each passing decade, it is obvious that centralized government continues to expand its tentacles into every part of our personal lives, all for the worse, along with horrific increases in taxes. Remember, dear sacred children of God, taxes confiscate the money we all earn for the benefit of ourselves and our families. We invest the sacred time that we have on earth to produce the necessary goods and services that benefit our families. Our government

---

[20] God's Grand Design, Blessed Mother Mary Speaks Directly Her Apparitions and The End of Times

has been confiscating what is really an increasingly deadly part of our existence: the time of our lives dedicated to our family. For every dollar the government confiscates, they have taken away that part of our sacred lives that we spent to earn it. It is accurate to say that all levels of government taxation including all the hidden ones that we have to pay when we buy groceries and gasoline to commute to and from work. On average, the taxes taken by all forms of government in total amount to approximately 45% to 53% of all earned personal income.

All of this is driven by people who are driven by Satanic impulses in the order of recklessly seeking more and more power over others of God's sacred children. They seek more and more money for themselves through clandestine means that are illegal but never accounted for. These are heinous sins against our loving Almighty God, and those who perpetrated all of this will certainly find their way through the gates of hell.

It is interesting that God will not condemn them to hell. Instead, after they all pass away, they will find themselves in front of our Lord and Savior, Jesus Christ. Their entire life will be displayed before them and measured against the magnificent Godly love and pure and perfect love that comes from The Trinity. They will see how rotten their behavior was when compared to Godly love. Then, with shrieking and gnashing teeth, they will realize nothing can be done. And the only path they have is through the gates of hell, and it is they who will condemn what they did during their lives.

At the proper time, all citizens of hell, including Satan Himself and all His demons, will be exposed to the rule that Jesus Christ calls the law of disintegration. All of hell will then start disintegrating back into nothingness from which it came. This includes the fact that there will not even be a memory in the minds of God's sacred children that everything in hell ever existed. Think about that.

26

To Stay in The Kingdom or Not

The Two Choices We All Must Make

There are two layers of these four choices, which are relatively easy to understand.

1. The first choice is to take the Earth Test or not.

    While we are spiritual beings within the Heavenly Kingdom, we must decide if we want to take the Earth Test or stay within the Heavenly Kingdom.

    All understand that if we choose the earth test, we are taking the risk of not coming back to the Heavenly Kingdom. But rather, we will be in hell and ultimately disintegrate back into the nothingness from which we came.

    However, there are great rewards if we go to Earth for the Earth Test. And coming back to the Heavenly Kingdom, there's something for grand celebration and the ability to have no restrictions on where you go or what you do in the Entire Kingdom.

2. The second choice of two: for those who are courageous enough and most of our Heavenly Father's sacred children are courageous enough to take the earth test. The Earth test will reveal the absolute inner workings of our entire spiritual being. We discover this by the way we lead our corporal lives on Earth. Satan has penetrated every aspect of life on earth, and we will be tempted and coerced every day of our human lives to be persuaded to sin against our Heavenly Father.

    If we are to succeed and return to the Heavenly Kingdom, we need to adhere to other parts of this book. This includes the Ten Commandments and the three manners of life that we must adhere to so that we qualify to go back into our Heavenly Father's Kingdom.

Lastly, I should remind everyone that within this book, there are detailed statistics of who gets back into heaven and who aren't based on their general positions within earthly societies. And religious beliefs along with political beliefs as well. For example, 0% of atheists make it back into the Heavenly Kingdom. Democrats versus Republicans within the United States. This information is pure and accurate because the source of this material and statistics is our Lord and Savior, Jesus Christ Himself. His knowledge is pure and perfect!

It has been said many times that each of us on earth has a choice to make: our Heavenly Father or Satan. It must be one or the other. There is no third choice. Every sacred child of God on earth must choose which one. How each sacred child conducts their life on earth demonstrates the choice we make, whether it is God or Satan, for all eternity. It also needs to be recognized that we do not fully understand the depths of our Spiritual being. Our Father has given us free will. What we say and do on earth is driven by the deepest parts of our Spiritual being and free will. What we create on earth will reflect what lies deeply within us. It is also a reflection of our free will, good or bad.

To discover what lies deep within us we must be tested in a fair manner so that we ourselves will know what is at the core of our being. So, almost all of you, God's children, choose to spend a life on earth which will test you to the very bottom of your existence. There will be suffering involved, and there will be attacks by Satan in many ways while you're on the earth. It is your response to these temptations and attacks that will demonstrate to you that you have decided to make of yourself.

Question: Were we, God's sacred children, compelled to be born on this earth for our redemption after the fall of Adam and Eve? Were we given a choice by our Father to stay in the Kingdom?

"My dearest son, you have asked a marvelous question. As you know, after you were created, you were given the same gift of free will that your Father also bestowed upon all His angels. As well as the love

between all the individuals that are part of all of God's creation. This also applies, my dear son, to creations that are beyond the ones that you know of. There are more.

<u>The situation before the Earth was habitable in its galactic development was that you and all of God's sacred children were such a loving and utterly endearing part of the Heavenly Kingdom. All of you were completely sinless. I must emphasize that all of you were incapable of any sin even though you possessed the wonderful gift of free will. However, when Satan rebelled against your Heavenly Father, everything changed. This event caused the potential for God's sacred children to also fall away from us in the Holy Trinity. This rebellion happened long before your Father created all of you, along with Adam and Eve and so on.</u>

Dear Lord: When was Lucifer's rebellion? Was it before or after God created all His sacred children?

Think about this through, dear son. Your Father knew long before we decided to create children in His image that Lucifer, one of His mighty angels, would rebel against Him in a horrifically sinful manner. <u>*Under no circumstances would God allow His sacred children to be exposed to Lucifer's evil while you were in the Heavenly Kingdom. Therefore, before you were lovingly created in your Father's image, Lucifer and His followers were cast out of the Heavenly Kingdom. Also, he was cast out long before the earth had developed to the point where it would support human life.*</u>

Potential Sacred Children Sin:

So, at some point in the vast history of your sacred existence, simultaneously, the conditions were that you were not created yet. Lucifer and his rebel angels were cast out of the Heavenly realm. Sent down to the pre-existing Spiritual realm, the part called hell made special for Satan and his demons. And to the earth where Lucifer now called Satan was forced to dwell with his angels now called demons. <u>*It was only after this that all of us in The Trinity engaged in the glorious*</u>

and loving creation of each one, each special and unique one of God's sacred children. You were then great citizens of the Heavenly realm where there was no conflict, where there was no Lucifer or rebellious angels.

There was no sin in the air, so to speak, that would tempt any of God's children. This is why every one of you was utterly sinless and was unable to succumb to temptation of any kind. All that potential sin was previously cast out of the Heavenly Kingdom when Lucifer and his angels were gone.

After that, because of Lucifer's pride bubbling up from deep inside him, it became unavoidable that you, in some manner in infinite time, would be exposed to sin within the multiple creations of Almighty God.

You may ask how could an angel created in perfection have such a negative emotion deep inside them? I will not go into all the details, but I will tell you that it has to do with the balance of all creations and the symmetry of everything in its totality. Remember, all God's children have no knowledge of everything else that occurs in created form from your Heavenly Father. There is the "other" that exists as well. That is all I want to tell you at this time.

All of this is a background to answer your first question: you were given a choice to come to the earth to be tested by your free will to choose your eternal destiny. Choose God for eternal paradise, living with The Trinity in the Heavenly Kingdom, and voluntarily obey the rules set forth for His children. Or choose to succumb to Satan's lure of false freedom and slowly dissolve back into nothingness from where everything associated with Satan will go.

Were all of God's children given a free choice whether to be born on the earth? Yes! God will never force Himself upon anything within all His creations. All have a choice.

Note: I did not know the following information until I got to writing this book for all of you, dear sacred children of our Almighty Father.

You, my dearest son, made your choice to live on the earth for a blink in time to resolve your eternal destiny. As I told you before, my dearest one, before you were born, you chose to live a life where you will always put others ahead of yourself. This is a remarkable choice while you were still within the Heavenly Kingdom. You wanted to emulate what is the essence of The Trinity. And so, you have lived such a life and you are yet to know and feel the glorious amount of love that is waiting for you when you return. You have suffered so much in the name of your Almighty Father.

All these choices are also available to every one of your Father's unique children. As it turns out, almost all of God's Spiritual children chose to live a life on earth. They wanted to be tested about their love for their Father and His ways. In this manner, everything that is deeply inside each child will be exposed to all to see, including themselves.

Often, even God's sacred children do not know or are aware of what lurks at the core of their free will. In a sense, you could call this a purification process for the benefit of all God's children and the physical and Spiritual realms. All of God's sacred children did know that if they had fatal free will flaws deep inside them, living within the Heavenly Kingdom would be torturous for them. This is because living a Holy life would seem like a prison to them sooner or later. They would rather know now by going to earth and finding out what boils inside them.

Free will is an overwhelmingly powerful gift to give to anyone. God did not want to create drones or robots. All of us in The Trinity wanted those children who love us with their own choice of free will. What pleasure is derived from being loved only because they were told to? That kind of love is an imposter and not love at all. This would fly into the face of the true character of the three of us in The Trinity. For as I said, while I was on earth, I am the way, the truth, and the life. It is the truth that makes everything work in such a loving manner. Without that, nothing is worth anything at all. It is the truth of each child's free will that guides their destiny one way or the other.

Now, what about the few of God's sacred children who were afraid to look inside themselves and go to earth to find out? Consistent with our deep love for all our children, they may stay inside the Heavenly Kingdom for all eternity. However, they will live freely in a restricted part of the Kingdom. Their lives will be glorious, filled with the love of us in The Trinity, of the angels, and of all the other children who preferred to stay in the Kingdom and not sojourn to earth. Their existence will indeed be joyous and excellent for all eternity. But they will do so in a much smaller and restricted part of the Heavenly Kingdom. All of us love them so very much that they will be ever so happy and do the things that they enjoy, whatever that may be.

My dear son, I hope that this answers your simple question. The answer, however, is complex yet simple at the same time. I hope I have given you an understandable context in which all of this occurs. I love you."

Yes! You certainly answered my question and gave all of us children much more beautiful information about the context in which this occurs. We all benefit from knowing so much more about our existence and how God's creations work together.

Those Who Choose Not to Go to Earth

Some of you will not choose to go to Earth because you do not want to risk never coming back to the Heavenly Kingdom. This choice is honored by your Father. In these cases, His children will remain within the Heavenly Kingdom. But they will be restricted in what they can do and where they can go. Your Heavenly Father will never permit anything that resembles sin or potential sin within the Heavenly Kingdom. So proper loving measures are taken to accommodate His children who choose not to take the Earth test. All of us in the Heavenly Kingdom completely understand this choice and honor all the children who choose this way.

There is never any embarrassment or second-class standing in doing this because the Heavenly Kingdom loves these children just as much as all the rest. This decision not to go to earth can be considered an incredible act of deep love for The Trinity. These children who choose this path do not want to risk in any way not being able to come back and live with their Heavenly Father in the Kingdom. This is viewed very positively. The others who go to Earth are viewed as wonderfully adventurous and want to show all creation their most profound love for their Heavenly Father and enjoy their eternal existence with The Trinity. They said the truth is that very many of God's sacred children succumb to the Satanic temptations on earth and do not return. All this decision-making is of everyone's free will. Nothing is forced upon any of our Father's children.

The following is a testimony from Almighty God regarding what I have just spoken about. These are the words of our loving Father when I asked Him about my encounter within the Heavenly realm and seeing my first grandchild preparing for her birth that was coming in a few months. Now, she is in college and is a bright student, and I am proud of her.

Question: What happens to each Spiritual child that comes to earth? What preparations are made while God's children are still in the Heavenly Kingdom before they are born into the world?

September 30, 2022, 9:46 AM

Before We Are Born on Earth, Extensive Preparation to Come Here

"It is a lengthy process, my dear son. There is no need to go into the selection process of who of God's Spiritual children will be next to the physical earth. That process is incredibly detailed and arranged to meet the needs and preferences of each child. This happens while they are in the Heavenly Kingdom after the selection process is completed and agreed that their coming life on the earth will satisfy the Spiritual needs of each child. And, after it is decided, their position and location on the earth will be fair.

A Major Decision for Our Personal Existence

<u>This means to reveal what their true feelings are. Like wanting to come back to the Heavenly realm for all eternity or choosing to be with Satan where there is no morality or any other fundamental behavioral standards that are to be met. Those who want that will choose Satan</u>

<u>with the understanding, they will, as you point out about entropy, they will slowly dissolve back into nothingness from which they came.</u>

After the selection process is completed to meet the individual needs of the children of God, they will then need to go through a preparation process. This includes many things, such as acclimatizing them for a life in the physical realm. Remember, none of God's children know what it is like to have been other than Spirit beings for their entire existence. They must get used, for example, not to have what they want instantaneously. They have to understand what hardship and Satanic dishonesty are because they have never experienced that either.

They will not understand the experience of dishonesty and other features of the disaster Satan has brought to the earthly realm. This is why little children on Earth believe everything they are told and are so gullible to all the falsity that exists on Earth.

It is only after each child feels comfortable enough with what is coming and the consequences that are involved regarding their fundamental decision of yes to God or yes to Satan. Only then will they be connected with their guardian angel, who will be with them throughout their physical existence. They will then come to know the family they will be born into and understand the general dynamics of family life on earth and the specific family they will be born into.

Nothing is left to chance. For this is always the way of your Father. Everything is perfectly planned with no random chances. After this reasonably long period of preparation then, they will decide at what point of their mother's pregnancy they will inhabit the physical baby developing in their mother's womb. This varies from child to child. During their mother's pregnancy, it is accurate to say that a child of God in the womb is a "developing human being" Blessed by the entire Trinity.

This is the general outline of what happens before a child of God is allowed to be born into the earthly realm. We all pray for each child as they leave so that they will pass the test of evil and return to us in the

Heavenly realm. This whole process will reveal what their true fundamental free will choice is.

It is only on earth that each child of God will completely understand themselves and why they make whatever choice they do. And lastly, they will decide a major theme of their life. Like you, my dear son, you chose your life as putting all other people ahead of yourself.

This is a very hard choice to make because it involves much suffering on the planet Earth. But you chose this, my dear son, before you were born on the earth. And I am so very proud of you, my dear son, for you have achieved Spiritual greatness that is not recognized by those around you. And now it is very good that you will include in this book the experience you had. When you visited your first granddaughter while she was at the last stages of preparation for her birth into the physical earth. I love you."

27

The Story of Me Seeing My First Granddaughter Before Her Birth

I know this story is completely true because it is directly from my personal experience. Approximately 23 years ago, I was anxiously anticipating the birth of my first grandchild. I was thrilled to know that I would soon be a grandfather. It turned out to be a girl. I was eager to hold her and tell my new grandchild that I love her. One afternoon, I was in my meditation room. As usual, the room was dark, and I had my earplugs in so as not to be distracted. I was sitting in my easy chair and thinking about my soon-to-be grandchild.

Suddenly, I felt as if I was leaving my body. The next thing I knew was in a tranquil room where lots of activity was happening. It was like a quiet hustle and bustle going on. I could hear the noise of Spirits shuffling around doing this, that, and other things. I am not sure really what they were doing. I could see many tiny Spiritual beings with the appearance of what I just described that God's children take before they are born into this physical world. They all look identical. You cannot tell them apart one from the other. Yet every Spirit child is unique, one of a kind. They were all the same size, and they were shuffling around. I was told that the Spirits I saw were all preparing for life on earth. What that entailed, I did not know.

One interesting note is that even though all these Spirit beings looked the same, they were not the same. They are all different and unique. Remember that each child of God is one of a kind, unique from all the rest. This means that every look-alike white Spirit being I saw had one-of-a-kind potential, fundamental personalities, interests, capabilities, and talents. All these differences are to be manifested in the baby after they are born. These characteristics of each child will grow in maturity over the years of life they have.

*NOTE: One day in prayer, I asked our Father why I have these Spiritual gifts when no one else I know has them to. He answered, **"It is because of the decision you made before you were born."** God, what did I say? God responded with these exact words: **"You decided that you would put all others before yourself. This is why you are gifted this way."** [21] My dear sacred children of our loving, Almighty Father, all of you had made a similar decision before you were born on Earth. First, you did not have to come to Earth. God never forces anything on His sacred children. But we are given choices, and this is what we did while all of us were still in the Heavenly Kingdom.*

Our options, as far as what general theme there will be in our lives on Earth is completely a free will choice given to us as a monumental loving gift from our Almighty Father. If you complain about your situation in life, remember that this is part of what you chose while you were still in the Heavenly Kingdom. Why did you choose what you did? The answer is the same for everybody. The answer is you and our Heavenly Father decided what were the best ways for each of us to grow spiritually. In such a manner that we will come closer and closer to the Heavenly Trinity, especially our Heavenly Father. Their rewards are great for doing that.

The Shape of Babies Still in The Spiritual Incubator of The Kingdom.

Every one of us, sacred children of God on Earth, were all babies developing within the Heavenly Kingdom. I was fortunate to witness this process, especially regarding my first grandchild, Isabella.

The form that all of them (the pre-born babies) take <u>looks very much like a semi-transparent very puffy pure white bowling pin</u>. But their upper body is bigger. They have two very small coal-black eyes and a small black nose. There were perhaps a few dozen of these "future baby" Spirits moving around. Then suddenly, one of these little Spirits came very close to me, possibly 18 inches or so. This Spirit being knew me somehow.

---

[21] Almighty God direct to me via telepathic communications

Yes, she knew who I was and kept looking at me. I instantly knew who she was, too. This little white Spirit was my first granddaughter about three months before she was due to be born to my daughter-in-law. I did not know what to say to her, and she said nothing in return. We just looked at each other, knowing who we were. After a while, it became awkward, and my visit to the Spiritual realm nursery came to an end, leaving me back in my meditation room, seated in my chair.

I sat in my chair for a while, pondering what just happened. I could not get over the fact that I was gifted ever so much to have this experience available to me. Without me asking, Almighty God knew what was on my mind and what I wanted to have happen. And consistent with His ways, God silently granted my prayer and that afternoon I made the trip, the instantaneous trip, to the Heavenly nursery where my first granddaughter was. My dear people, think very much about this kind of event because it is a normal thing to happen in God's creation.

28

The Historical Percentages of Different Groups Living Today Who Make It Back into Heaven.

Jesus Christ
January 5, 2024- January 9, 2024

Question: My dear Lord and Savior, recently, I watched a video on a YouTube that quoted several well-known clergies, bishops, and others of the Catholic Church. These the people who, in mid-evil times where they collectively revealed just how few terribly few numbers of God's sacred children would be qualified to live within the Holy Kingdom of Heaven after they passed away. This bothered me greatly because the percentage of people is never more than 1% or 2%. This bothers me immensely. My dearest, loving Lord and Savior, I know we discussed this point before, and you told me it was more like 30%. Could you please provide more detailed information on this question? Thank you, dear Lord.

Yes, my dearest son, I know that video bothered you immensely. It is because you love so much the others of God's sacred children, and to think that almost all are going to hell is very painful for you.

The answer you are seeking is when you take the entire world's population into account, it is what I previously told you, approximately 30%. But if we were to break that down into different pieces, it would be something like this: **The Major Religions in The World As of 2010**

Christians

32% of the World Population 2.4 billion

60% Make It Back into The Kingdom

For Christians or from those who claim they are Christians in their lives when interacting with others of God's sacred children, approximately 60% only. This is because a lot of people that call themselves Christian really do not practice Christianity in their daily lives therefore, they are more secular and ignore the beauty of Christianity. Many people within the community of avowed Christianity, we could say that they are Christians in name only, and they live secular lives. They are the ones who don't attend church, and if they do, it's usually when their conscience prompts them to make up for a recent absence. A sense of guilt comes over them regarding this.

There are Christians who have turned secular in many ways. They follow, to one extent or another, the Satanic and paganistic ways of life and believe much of the propaganda that Satan spews out into the world. These are the ones who, through various levels of ignorance of their religion, are passive regarding abortion and that it is conscious and willful murder of developing sacred children of your Father. This is pure Satanic.

There are so many ways that Christians can dilute and extinguish Christianity in their lives. Such that they do it so slowly they don't even notice. It is like mold growing on their Spiritual selves that ultimately chokes them to death.

These are the ones that, when I said the parable of spreading the seeds, fall on marginal places that give them Christian beliefs. But due to a variety of conditions, they grow somewhat but then wither away. Regarding these situations, a Christian must first take a self-introspection of their Christian beliefs, what a real Christian believes in, and how a Christian behaves in His life.

Advise From Our Lord and Savior Jesus Christ About Self Introspection

Take an honest assessment and identify where you feel you've gone wrong. Then, knowing your Heavenly Father is merciful and forgiving, confess what you believe are your sins. Admit them to your Heavenly

Father, to remember your Father is also within you because he loved every one of His sacred children so much that he left part of Himself within our Spiritual bodies. So, there is absolutely no way that your Father does not hear everything you say in your life, especially everything you address to Him. After you confess your sins, ask for God's forgiveness and guidance so that you stop doing whatever you feel is sinful. If you think something is immoral, it is because you have not connected with your Father within and with His Holy rules for human life on Earth.

Remember, dear sacred child, the Holy Trinity already knows what your sins are. So, when you confess your sins, you tell your Heavenly Father you are now aware of what you may have done wrong. And that is a wonderful thing because that opens the door to continue walking the path, the Heavenly path back to Heaven from where you came.

From that moment on, you have grown wonderfully within the Heavenly Spirit. Ask for forgiveness from the bottom of your heart, say the act of contrition prayer, and then ask for Godly advice and guidance in everything you do from that point on. Along the path to Heaven, increase the frequency of your prayers to your Father and me and the Holy Spirit. You can see The Trinity if you wish. Say your prayers sincerely because that makes all the difference in the world. Mechanical prayers mean nothing. They must come from your inner soul, your inner heart. In this way, you will grow spiritually in the proper direction, which, in the end, is the Heavenly Kingdom for you.

If you have read this book and made a conscious effort to understand what Richard has written in my words, then you will have succeeded in correcting your path. And now you are on the path to your Heavenly Father and the Kingdom.

Priests and Nuns

	1950's	*1960's*
Priests:	*84%*	*64%*
Nun's	*75%*	*73%*

I feel like asking this question is almost sacrilegious and insulting to the clergy. Having observed the Catholic Church over the last 50 years and kept in touch with the Vatican, I've noticed since Vatican II, the church appears to be drifting away from its original foundational theologies. In my previous book, co-written with our Blessed Mother Mary, she exposes how badly our beloved Catholic Church, and especially the Vatican, has allowed a lot of Satanic activity within the Vatican itself. Additionally, there are many now bishops and Cardinals who actively worship Satan. I find this horrifically disgusting.

If you are a typical Christian believer, what I just said is horrifying and shocking. It was for me when our Blessed Mother Mary, while writing her book on her apparitions and the End of Times. If you want more details on this and many other highly relevant topics for the times we live in, get a copy of our book titled "God's Grand Design: Blessed Mother Mary Reveals Her Apparitions and The End of Times."

Question: Proceeding onward, my dear lord and Savior Jesus, it would be exceptionally good if everybody knew the truth about just how close to God our priests and nuns are. I suspect that over the last 50 years, there has been an increasing number of priests who have fallen away but remain in the priesthood. It would be helpful to compare the current times in 2024 against The Historical 1950s. I say that because the End of Times began in the 1960s.

What a marvelous question, my dear son. I do know the answer for both the times you specify, and both of us are very saddened and what is happening in our beloved Catholic Church, especially the Vatican.

WARNING!

My Personal Notation: Most sincere Christians believe that, among other minor changes, Vatican II made the way we receive the Holy Eucharist. Now the Catholic Church shall distribute the most important part of the Mass, the Eucharist, by simply handing it out like an advertising pamphlet. Rather than on our tongue, which is a pure way in which recognizing the sanctity and the fact that Jesus Christ is the one that reconnected God's sacred children with our Heavenly Father. <u>This is completely wrong and a result of satanic guidance from the Vatican</u>. As for me, I will not allow a priest to hand out the holy Eucharist like a pamphlet. Rather, it will be on my tongue, or I will walk away after scolding the priest for not doing what Jesus has instructed us to do.

Jesus Christ
January 5, 2024:

As you correctly mentioned, <u>Vatican II was the initial start of the liberalization and secularization of our beloved church. It was a giant move away from the church I found 2000 years ago.</u>

As prophesied many times, which can be found in Biblical literature, our beloved Catholic church will suffer great intrusions and invasions by people who are gravely attached to Satan, and they will do His will. This of course means increasing sinful pollution in all levels of our church. This Satanic invasion into the church will accelerate as time goes on, as was prophesied by our Blessed Mother Mary in her apparitions at Fatima in 1917.

One sign that Our Catholic Church has been thoroughly invaded by Satan is that Pope Francis, on two separate occasions, purposely and willfully lied about the contents of Mother Mary's third apparition at Fatima. People believe that the Pope never lies. However, he certainly did and misled every Christian on Earth. He even went so far as to say that the third secret did not exist, which is exposed in your book written with you and Blessed Mother Mary. Frankly, there are extremely few people that know the real third secret of Fatima. **I am ever so happy** that you and Mother Mary wrote the book you mentioned earlier because: It is the only book in existence that contains the real 3rd secret of Fatima.

Jesus Christ
October 2024

The reason the pope lied about this so-called secret of Fatima is because it reveals terrible information regarding the church, regarding POPE FRANCIS, and exposes all Satanic activity going on in the Christian religious realm.

All this bad news being said, looking back into the decade of the 1960s, it is that 80% of the clergy, including the nuns, made it back into Heaven. The decision criteria for entering the Kingdom are a little harder for priests and nuns. Because they will also be judged on how well they carried out their responsibilities in ministering to Christians and other people whom they have vowed to serve. Some of the clergy did not live up to that.

As you have observed, my dear son, things have worsened within our church over time, and the numbers are consequently worse. As of now, only 64% of the clergy, taken as a whole, will return back to the Heavenly Kingdom. This is what has been prophesied by a number of people including our Blessed Mother Mary when she spoke to you and co-wrote the book you mentioned above. The world must go through the tribulations that have been described in the third secret of Fatima before I will return to Earth. You, my son, will be with me before then and I want you to be with me during my return—the second coming.

I love you so very much.

Summary

	1950s	*2020*
Priests	*84%*	*64%*
Nuns	*75%*	*73%*

In the decade of the 1950s, this was before the End of Times began. You are ever so right, my dear son, the event that kicked off the End of Times was when Lyndon Baines Johnson created and passed the bill through your Congress named <u>The Great Society</u>. Democrats always put a title on their congressional bills that are complete lies. Like the one currently passed by your Biden administration titled <u>The Inflation Reduction Act</u>. It spends billions more on money that does not exist, which can only increase inflation, yet they call it decreasing.

These are Satanic lies to the ignorant American people. Johnson's Great Society Act demanded that the man of a home must leave his entire family to qualify for government financial assistance. This is an entirely disgusting Satanic demand that breaks apart the sacred structure of what God intended for all His sacred children. In a very Satanic way, he purposely destroyed the will of God, which is "families shall be with one wife and one husband." Through lies of the Tonkin Gulf incident, he also created the Vietnam War, which resulted in hundreds of thousands of deaths of God's sacred children. He is now a leader in hell. And like all people in hell, ultimately, he will be dissolved back into nothingness from whence he came.

The 1960s was also a turning point where the government started to expand at an increasingly rapid rate, putting its hands around the necks of God's sacred children. The lower numbers of those going to Heaven for the clergy in 2020 is a direct result of the moral degradation within your society, which cannot help but also affect our beloved clergy. The scandals of priests doing unthinkable things to the vulnerable are hateful Satanic behavior. Enough said.

Judaism

.2% of the World Population 14 million

43% Make It Back into The Kingdom

Thank you for asking, dear son. Judaism is very much like Christianity in the fundamentals. The Old Testament is what these people of God relate to the most. Most Hebrews do not believe that I am their lord and savior. Their focus is on the Historical Old Testament, which started, of course, with Abraham.

Judaism has a lot in common with Christianity. However, I am the dividing line in that Judaism does not recognize me as the savior and Lord of God's sacred children on Earth. These Children of God are stuck in the idea that their history defines how they should live their lives today and their Historical beliefs of 3,000 years ago. This is a serious problem that hinders their Spiritual growth, especially considering that I came to Earth to save all the Jewish people as well as everybody else. That history drives their modern lives today can be observed with the rules regarding what is kosher or not. This supplies the ideas around food preparation and the food itself.

Go to a food market in the Jewish section of a city, you'll find signs saying kosher, which means the food is consistent with Old Testament rules of what can be eaten or not. For example, the Jewish people should never eat pork. It is not kosher. Why it is because historically, pork was a source of a disease called trichinosis. They learned this in Old Testament times, so they banned it from being consumed by the Jewish people. Now, however, pork is safe to eat, but since it is not kosher, Jewish people avoid it.

People do not remember that I was born a Jew and that I died on the cross as a Jewish rabbi. One would think that since I spent my entire life within the Jewish community, I would be more highly revered in their beliefs. The Jewish people knew very well that I was resurrected, and I appeared to many people after my death on the cross.

However, again, the Jewish people unknowingly live primarily by the laws of life as handed down by your Heavenly Father. They are at the foundation. They are reasonable and loving people. As you know, my dearest son and I have told several people the reason the Jews are singled out for horrific crimes against them. It is because deep down inside those people who are Satanically oriented, they automatically hate the Jewish people. After all, they are the chosen ones of your Heavenly Father.

So now come back to your original question of what percentage of the Jewish people reach the Heavenly Kingdom. The answer is that 43% of the Jewish nation made it back to the Heavenly Kingdom from whence they came, as so did everybody on Earth. Thank you for asking this question. It is a beautiful one. It digs deep into the truth of the condition of the Spiritual lives of people on Earth.

Just as it is now with the war going on as you write this fantastic book, it all started with a group of Muslims that invaded southern Israel. They slaughtered way more than 1000 innocent people simply going about their day-to-day activities. You know of the telephone call from one of the terrorist criminals when he called his mother and bragged that he had killed 10 Jews with his bare hands. This is pure Satan if anybody wants to think about it objectively. Worse yet, the entire Muslim people celebrated the deaths of so many innocent Jewish people. Every war that goes on that involves Israel always follows the same pattern. Somebody within the Muslim communities, their leaders, find a reason, ample or most times small, that is manufactured within their Satanic hearts and then want another war with the Jewish nation. Never once has the nation of Israel purposely attacked another country so they could dominate them. On the other hand, Muslim nations do this as a regular course of business.

I love you, my dearest son. Thank you so much for applying your massive skills in writing and communicating to God's sacred children all the information we give you about your Father's and my creations, especially His sacred children on Earth.

Islam/Muslims

1.6 billion, 23% of The World Population

6% Make It Back into The Kingdom

Islam IS The Religion of Satan. Also, The Democrat Party Is the Political Arm of Satan In Our Beloved United States of America

Its foundations are based on domination, fear, and hatred. Everywhere Muslims go on the earth, hate, chaos, social conflict, along with wars with everybody who is not a Muslim will shortly follow behind. If you do not believe this, go to some objective statistics and find out for yourself. These statistics and data are provided later in this book.

All my life, starting in the 1950s, I have always heard about "unrest in the Middle East." Why? It is because Islam will kill anybody who does not submit to Islamic domination. All of this is described in detail within the Quran rather than the Hadith or Sunnah. Wars will increase, and this will be accompanied by increasingly severe natural disasters. All of this will happen far worse than people can imagine. These constant wars are events that politicians like to blame on climate change. John Kerry likes to run around the earth in his polluting private jet, spreading false scientific information, which it is not. He tries to boost his fake climate change theory that it is caused by human beings. **John Kerry is a self-centered, power-hungry, ignorant stooge for Satan** by distracting the good and honest Godly people on the Earth toward fake climate change science. The climate change scam is yet another way that Satan uses to enslave God's sacred children into a false way of life, worshipping Gia and the atmosphere as a god.

When examining the data, the fatal error that Kerry purposely prefers to make is associating the very loosely connected bits of data that have been hand-selected by Kerry in a highly unscientific manner. In other words, John Kerry looks for data that only supports his preconceived notions of the points he wishes to make. That is as far away from real science as you can get.

Please remember, dear sacred reader, I hold degrees in chemistry and physics and was a scientist at NASA Ames Research Center, where I conducted upper atmospheric research using complex instrumentation, commonly known as electron microscopes. They were connected to spectrophotometers and so on. They would count the results from the various wavelengths that determined the elementary composition of the particles we collected with U-2 spy planes at approximately 80,000 feet above ground.

Think about it: John Kerry has no idea regarding the complex analysis I did that shows he doesn't know what he's talking about. He amounts to no more what I would call a "Chicken Little", always running around screaming that the sky is falling.

Satan hates God's sacred children, so the temperature goes up by 1.5°, and everybody will die by noon. To relate this awful mess to real life, remember that across the world, temperatures from breakfast to lunch increase by at least 10 to 15 degrees, which scares Kerry's butt off. <u>Kerry is an atheist. It's easy to see in order to be consistent with the hate of Satan, it is God's sacred children that must be blamed for naturally cyclical temperature variations around the Earth.</u> To refute John Kerry's loosely patched-together statistics, please look up something called the Milankovitch Cycles.

This is where things get tricky. If a person is born a Muslim, the only worldview that they are taught is one of dominion and hatred. They are taught that women are second-class citizens. They are taught to kill and kill again. This, however, does not mean that all Muslims go to hell. Many Muslims use their built-in sense of love for other human beings which was built into them before they were born. Many Muslims follow their instincts and reject what their leaders tell them, but they must do this silently. You have said that many times.

<u>*Islam Is A Manifestation of Satan On Earth*</u>*. You hit the nail on the head, my dear son. Islam thrives on hatred and fear. This is built into Muslim societies. Basically, it is you will believe in the false god Allah that I tell you to believe in, or I will kill you. This is both pure hatred and pure fear. This is exactly how Satan rules His Kingdom.*

Their ultimate goal is to control the entire world and dominate everyone in it, which is exactly the opposite of what your Heavenly Father wants. This in and of itself is the highest form of Satanic action.

This is a demonstration of how much Satan hates your Heavenly Father, Me, the Holy Spirit, and all Christians such as yourself. As we talked about earlier, <u>Islam Is the Religion of Satan,</u> and this is why there will never be peace in the Middle East. And as you have said, dear son, you have observed war after war when the Muslims always find a reason, no matter how small, to attack God's chosen people. This stems from the foundational hate that Satan has developed against your Heavenly Father. This applies especially to all Christians and all the other sacred children of God on Earth.

This is why only 6% of Muslims make it into Heaven. It is only those that successfully found their inner being. And found your Heavenly Father's laws of life imprinted in every one of His sacred children with before they came to earth, dear son, yes, only 6% of Muslims make it to the Heavenly Kingdom. It makes me extremely sad to say that.

Irreligion

6% 14 million

1% Make it Back into The Kingdom. This includes such "religions" such as: Baha'i faith, Jainism, Sikhism, Shintoism, Taoism, Wicca, and Zoroastrianism.

Question: Dear Lord Jesus, is it appropriate to include in this category the various folk or traditional religions, including African traditional religions, Chinese folk religions, Native American religions, and Australian aboriginal religions?

Yes, my dear son, that is the best as you can do with the data, which can be confusing at times. But it does give our sacred children a good idea of how the proportions of people on earth are represented.

Thank you for asking this, my dear son. This term refers to a diverse range of miscellaneous religious beliefs that are grouped together. Some people believe that nature on Earth is a god of sorts. Other people believe that the Earth gives all life and is a god. Some people look up to the sky, see the universe, and therefore think the physical universe is

God. Some people believe that human beings are gods, which gets back to Greek theology, where everything under the Sun could be called a god.

Frankly, my dearest son, this does irritate me because people like this do not bother to search more deeply into themselves or ask the question where all of this came from. This is the most short-sighted category on the face of the Earth. I am irritated because these sacred children of God never bother to look past the end of their noses.

So fundamentally, dear son, you can categorize these people as the ones that worship everything. To answer your question directly about the percentage of this kind of people that make it into the Heavenly Kingdom, the answer is only 7%. This is very much like the hostile and rage-filled Satanic Muslims on Earth today. These kinds of people reinforce their beliefs by going out into nature and being mesmerized by the beauty of it all. Fundamentally, they are worshiping your Heavenly Father's creation but not your Heavenly Father who created it.

Hinduism

1.2 billion 15% of Earth's Population

18% Make It Back into The Kingdom

The percentage of Hindus that make it into Heaven is 18%. In their belief system, they refer to a god, but it is not the correct and actual God creator of all that is seen and unseen. It is more like a god that supervises only the earth. The few people I mentioned are open to a more enormous God that goes beyond Hindu belief. It is in this way they are responding to the Godly heart within their Spiritual being that was placed there for every one of God's sacred children. Remember, my dear son, when all sacred children are born to Earth, a fundamental understanding of God's laws for life are imparted within them.

Hindus take physical life as it is but do not really question in any depth who made everything. In this respect, they are very short-sighted, but they have a code of living ethics that is very constructive and misguided. Remember, in Hinduism, they believe that cows are their dead relatives. Therefore, cows are sacred in addition to cows being spiritually responsible for other minor beliefs as well.

Within Hinduism you will hear the following four items which are all central to the belief system of Hindus. Please notice that there is no reference to a god that created all that is seen and unseen. Hinduism seems to take for granted the existence of the world and the universe with no reference to who created it. To me, your author, it appears as if life boils down to a merry-go-round with no end in sight. How depressing is that?

Other Hindu Beliefs

1. Hinduism is also centered around the idea of reincarnation. People must repeatedly relive their lives again and again until they reach the state of Nirvana.
2. Hinduism believes in Karma. This is the belief that people are rewarded or punished in one incarnation according to their deeds in the previous incarnation.
3. Hinduism believes in Samsara which refers to the endless series of births deaths and rebirths to which all beings are subject.
4. Hinduism believes in the Atman which is the soul of the world from which all individual souls are derived and to which they return as the supreme goal of existence.

Buddhism

7% 14 million People on Earth

27% Make It Back into The Kingdom

My dear son, you know the story of how Buddhism began. Siddhartha Gautama was purposely sheltered by his royal family and was never allowed to leave the walls of the palace which was quite large. He was treated with all the finery and delicious foods that were available at the time for the very wealthy. As he grew older, you know, he became very curious about what lay on the other side of the walls that had contained him for so long.

So, he left the palace grounds and started to walk through the various towns and cities that were relatively close by. He was utterly horrified at what he found where the people were suffering terribly from diseases, from missing limbs, with blisters and all other sorts of skin diseases, plagues and so on.

For quite some time, he had wanted to be by himself and bring to the people a code of conduct and a belief in a central god of sorts. He developed interpersonal relationship laws. And from his limited understanding of God and The Trinity, did the best to bring peace to the minds of the people and establish a code of conduct. A code that would help them organize the production of food and other daily necessities. He did the best he could with what he had, and the people loved Him for it.

He traveled the country as a Holy man. He felt that the truth of life would be found within the Spirit of every person. Therefore, he meditated a lot, and as the story goes, he gained Nirvana, which is enlightenment or, said differently, knowledge of the Spiritual realm connecting with the physical. He then became known as <u>***The Buddha, Which Means the Enlightened One.***</u>

What Buddha was doing was trying to communicate with his own spiritual being, which does contain fundamental rules of life your Heavenly Father placed in every one of His sacred children before they were born. The Buddha had every good intention of relieving the suffering, specifically the physical suffering, of the people in the land.

How many Buddhists are believed to enter Heaven? They believe they can with their peaceful nature and introspection. They try seeking the truth of Almighty God, they do live mostly in accordance with what you have published many times regarding the laws of life from your Almighty Father. However, few succeed. They are, in a very real sense are worshiping the godly part of themselves not Almighty God creator of Heaven and Earth, of all that is seen and unseen. So yes, many of them do make it into Heaven, and the percentage is 27%. You may think the number should be higher because of their peaceful nature but most Hindus do not pursue the truth that God has set forth within themselves. They respond to their physical instincts much more than you would guess.

Those who do make it into Heaven will be given a choice because of the merciful and loving nature of your Almighty Father. As you explained earlier in your magnificent book, the choice will be to stay in Heaven and be with the others who chose not to come to Earth to take the Earth test. The other choice is to be born again on Earth to take the full Earth test. If they choose to stay in Heaven, they will be enormously loved, and life will be like a paradise for everyone. They, of course, like everyone in Heaven, will have the ability to improve over time and rise higher within the Heavenly Kingdom.

Other Groups Not a Direct Religious Organized Faith

Atheists/Agnostics

7% 450 - 500 million

0% Make It Back into The Kingdom

These are simply people who deny the existence of Almighty God or have serious doubts whether God exists or not. Atheists and agnostics don't realize that because they are a sacred child of God and our He exists within them, when they deny the existence of God, they also denying their own existence as well.

Question: Dear Lord Jesus, this category to me has two aspects to it. Of course, the first and most important one is the percentage of nonbelievers that make it back to the Kingdom. But also, this brings up a question about last-minute conversions to Christianity when these atheist people are extremely close to death having lived all their life already. If they scream and yell and holler and say, "oh my God I'm so sorry I'm awful I know I am headed to hell, but dear Lord I now understand please forgive me."

My dear son, that is a beautiful question. First, you already know the answer that nobody that denies the existence of our Heavenly Father can possibly enter the Heavenly Kingdom. So, the answer numerically is 0%.

The far more interesting question is what is normally referred to as a deathbed realization and asking for forgiveness and admission to the Heavenly Kingdom. Remember, my dear son, that your Heavenly Father is very merciful and forgiving and he does want every one of His sacred children to come back to Him in the Heavenly Kingdom. So, the question is how bad was their life on Earth? An extreme example is those causing great damage to others of God sacred children than does a deathbed confession and begging for forgiveness cancel out everything they did to damage others of God sacred children?

This is a very hard question to answer because on one hand you have a merciful and forgiving Father yet at the same time this person by all measurements and standards should go to hell. Like this, they completely failed to live by the behavioral standards of your Heavenly Father. This is to love Almighty God first above everything else, to love your neighbor as you love yourself, and to even love your enemy. People like this put their Satanic tendencies repeatedly above loving their Almighty Father. That is not canceled out by saying a few words out of the fear of death.

To enter the Heavenly Kingdom, the proof of belief in Almighty God is demonstrated by how they lived their life. That is overwhelming evidence of their rejection of us, Almighty God, for their entire life. Their very fundamental nature is controlled by Satanic impulses and playing out those impulses in real life against other sacred children. Knowing things that they will pass away very soon only motivates them through fear of saying the words, forgive me. Please allow me into the Kingdom. It is not love for their Heavenly Father. The only fear is so overwhelming they will say anything and do anything to avert their destiny into hell.

Your Almighty Father is also a fair and loving judge of His sacred children. In cases like this, we must consider the fundamental purity and love that each person has at the bottom of their heart, which must be demonstrated throughout their life. In cases like this, the answer is <u>no! They will not be admitted to the Heavenly Kingdom.</u> And hell is their only destination. They will realize and come to understand in a pure and perfect environment of love that everyone experiences right after they pass away, they will realize that there is no place for them in Heaven. Ultimately, if they are in the Kingdom, their fundamental Satanic behaviors will come back to the surface and be very detrimental to everyone else within the Kingdom. That is never allowed. To use Hitler as an example, none of our sacred children would ever believe that people like Him would end up in the Heavenly Kingdom.

So, my dearest son, in <u>conclusion it is how a person lives their life that is the ultimate demonstration of who and what they really are, and it is that which determines their ultimate destiny.</u> The Heavenly realm is perfect and pure, and nobody will be allowed in unless they have demonstrated their love for Almighty God.

Thank you, my dear Lord and Savior. I know that every believing person on earth will understand this thoroughly because it makes such great sense. It is easy to see your immense love for all your sacred children on earth within every answer you gave to my questions. I love you, dear Lord.

The Two Political Parties in The United States

A few years ago, I wrote a book titled **"Christian's Alert! Democrats are attacking our country."**

17% of Democrats Make It Back into The Kingdom

4% of Democrat Leaders Make It Back into The Kingdom

Dear Lord Jesus, I certainly know that this is an odd request, but through my lifelong observations, I feel very strongly that **<u>The Democrat Party is Indeed the Political Arm of Satan</u>**. This identification of the Democratic Party was not entirely accurate when I was a little boy in the

1950s. What started to go haywire in the 1960s and grew like a deadly disease into the Satan worshiping party that it really is today. So, my dearest Lord, please comment on the percentage of Democrats that make it into Heaven. I believe I already know the reasons for the ones that do not reasons for those that do.

My dearest son, this is a magnificent question and is so relevant to what your country, America, is suffering under right now. The very existence of America is in grave danger. Danger of dissolving into the death of the country and the dissolution of all its citizens into continual warring groups in their Satanic pursuit of power and money. There will be flowing blood in the streets, as the history of the United States today will come to a grinding halt of pain and suffering. As you already know my dear son this was prophesies multiple times in the Holy Bible by several different prophets.

So, as you can imagine, it depends upon each person who identifies as a Democrat just how far down the hole of sin they demonstrated in their life. On average, however, only 17% of Democrats make it into the Heavenly Kingdom. It is those people who are sincerely interested in making better the lives of those who are suffering emotionally or financially or within society. However, if you were to ask me what percentage of Democrat leaders would go to Heaven, it would be far less than the average 17%. Much lower.

Okay, my dearest Lord, what is the percentage of Democrat leaders that make it into Heaven?

It is good that you asked me. The percentage is exceedingly low. It hovers around 3% to no more than 4%. Another reason for this awful statistic results from their Satanic activities to do anything and everything without any morals or ethics to gain political power and money.

Obviously, dear son, you remember back in the 1950s when both parties would huddle together and make budget decisions and come to a compromise solution that would be fair and just for everyone. I know that you remember Everett Dirksen, a Democrat leader back in the 1950s, and how he was so open to honoring different views on issues. He made honest negotiations to come to a common answer where everybody got part of what they wanted and surrendered to the other party they could live with that had understanding and compassion behind it.

Over the years, as you have observed that you are correct that the End of Times began in the 1960's with Lyndon Baines Johnson's presidency. His Great Society bill was nothing like what the Democrats advertised to the people. The most heinous thing against God was the requirement that the husband in a black family to get financial support from the government had to leave his home. This is pure Satan in action. The black community has never been the same ever since. Their suffering has been magnified many times over. Satan always wanted to destroy the family structure; he knows without a father in the home, the children are deprived of the important guidance, strength, and discipline Fathers are supposed to provide for their children. Satan knew that this would lead to many more problems that have now manifested themselves into violence everywhere you look and the complete lack of any sense of responsibility and moral justice.

Satan has successfully turned the black community into a violent jungle. Even the black community's music reflects the domination of one group over another or sexual innuendos that anything goes. As you already know, it was painful for me to even look at Him when he came to me for his final judgment. He is now a leader in Satan's hierarchy of leaders in hell.

As you know, my dear son the Kamala Harris presidential bid is really based on nothingness. There is no constructive substance to anything she has said, with the exception she has most recently adopted some policies she was totally against, just a few years ago. She adopted them directly from Donald Trump in his plan for the betterment of the United States. This is about as dishonest as you can get, and you are right, my dear son, when you have observed Kamala Harris has never once received a vote for any office she wanted to get. She is the ultimate in a political puppet that will be controlled by sin and the Satanic command of Barack Obama.

Other Satanic Democrat leaders include Hillary Clinton, Bill Clinton, the communist Bernie Sanders, the communist Alexandra Ocasio Cortez. Also, the completely dishonest Nancy Palosi, who recently became a serious alcoholic, the marginally intelligent political puppet Pete Buttigieg. Finally, Alejandro Mayorkas who has done tremendous damage to the sacred children in the United States. This was done by allowing horrific numbers of illegal aliens into your country. The damage they will do is just beginning, dear son, along with the Democrat party's efforts to turn the illegals into voting people, and the list goes on.

I'm sure you know, my dear son, that these people are power seekers at the expense of the American people, who are precious, sacred children of your Heavenly Father. Their lifetime behavior and anti-God attitudes will undoubtedly lead them directly to hell. It will be very unpleasant for me to inform them of their eternal destiny. This makes me so sad I could cry, but this is what they have decided to do of their own free will, with the gift your Heavenly Father gave them, and that is the consequence.

Lastly, my dear son, you summed up the situation very well in your book titled "America Alert, The Democrats Are Attacking Our Country." I love you, my dear son.

Republicans

Republicans 67% Make It Back into The Kingdom

Republican Leaders 53% Make It Back into The Kingdom

Dearest Lord Jesus, it is my personal conviction that many more Republicans will be entering the single gate into the Heavenly Kingdom. Yes, there are goofballs and power-hungry politicians within the Republican Party. They, like everyone else, want to feel secure in their life and their political position. These individuals often engage in illicit activities and make unauthorized deals with whomever they deem suitable. However, the Republican Party is sincerely in love with the American dream that is found in our Constitution and our Bill of Rights. These individuals are primarily God-centered and strive to do what they can within the political realm to promote the best interests of the American people. They are generally not seeking more power over the people, unlike the Democrats. I hope I'm correct in this, dear Lord. Please share your thoughts with all your children who read this.

Oh, my dearest son, I love what you just said. Frankly, it does accurately reflect the current state. I didn't do that of the Republican Party. I'm proud of you for that. Like all human organizations, there are many faults to be found, yet they are far more seekers of truth than seekers of power and money like Democrats. These individuals are deeply concerned about the health, wealth, and safety of the American people. However, it is tough for them to break through the false images that the Democrats try to paint within the minds of the American people.

The presidential run of Pres. Donald Trump will be successful. This is what I told you before when you wrote down what I said regarding his assassination attempt that was orchestrated by leaders in the Democrat party along with the FBI and the Secret Service. It was all created by 12 Democrats and Democrat appointees.

To answer your question my dear son directly, I would like to put it in the same format as the Democrats. That is regular Republicans and Republican leaders.

For Republican people living in America, the percentage on average is 67% that make it into Heaven. However, like in the case of the Democrat Party, the leaders of the Republican Party have risen to the top mostly by performing dishonest shenanigans, underhanded deals, and other political maneuvers along with hidden briberies.

As you have noticed, there is an enormous difference between Republican voters and Democrat voters. There are lots of reasons for this. People in the Democrat Party could be accurately described as high school students who carry with them many times bad attitudes and are angry within themselves. This is fertile ground for Satan to tempt them successfully in many ways. They are generally selfish in nature but have learned how to successfully lie to people by proposing something that will benefit the people.

They are, by their nature, generally very interested in power and money, much more so than Republican voters. Democrats are far more likely not to worship Almighty God and instead do something else that involves entertainment. Democrats are very good at making excuses for themselves for not doing or doing something that is either destructive or is in some fashion helpful for them to meet their goals of money and power. Democrats are generally considered less trustworthy than Republicans.

Average Republicans are more likely to attend church, contribute to worthy causes, and salute the American flag. <u>There are far more Democrats in jail and prison than there are Republicans.</u>

Males/Females

Males: 37% Make It Back into The Kingdom

Females: 63% Make It Back into The Kingdom

My dearest Lord Jesus, these two groups of God's sacred children will prove to be extremely interesting. I believe, controversial given the false definitions of what a woman is and so much ego and pride in both sexual categories as defined by our Heavenly Father.

You are so very right, my dear son. In recent years, there has been a purposeful and constant blending of the two genders. This is to undermine the independent yet complementary roles that each gender plays in supporting one another, as designed by your Heavenly Father. As I mentioned earlier, it certainly takes one of each gender to properly and successfully raise their children. A woman is intended to bear the family's children, tend to their physical needs, and provide the necessary meals and nurturing for all the family's children.

As technology has increased, especially over the last 50 years, the advance of great labor-reducing products and a host of other convenience items, all of this has reduced greatly the workload to run a household. It used to be a 24-hour-a-day load on the woman of the house. Long hours of hand-washing clothes, preparing foods from a more natural state and without processing, and so on.

This resulted in much extra time for the woman of the house to expand their activities into the workplace. This is actually very good because now there can be two sources of income if the family chooses. This also means that the family can spend more time together over the weekend and take vacations together. This is a wonderful thing. Recently, because of ever-growing demands placed on us (taxes and regulations) driving up prices, it's now a necessity for both mother and father to work just to provide the necessities of life.

Over many years of smaller government, it took only one middle-class job to support the entire family. The advent of government passing out more and more benefits to certain groups of people in the name of charity. Other reasons this has the force and effect of more and more financial slavery to all those who work for a living to support their families. This is a form of enslavement where the government constantly confiscates more and more of the fruits of the laborers of both husband and wife. All of this is in the name of benefits where everything could have been afforded directly by the wage earners family without government intervention and extra costs to pay government wages.

The government has slowly transformed from serving the people to dominating the people and regulating every detail of God's sacred children's lives in your country. Additionally, in the last 50 years more of your Democrat politicians feverishly seek more political power and money. They force upon citizens a communist lifestyle which gives the government absolute power over everybody, and freedom becomes just a distant memory.

To answer your question directly, because women are less exposed to the ways of the world due to raising children, it is 63%. Women are the nurturing and caregiving members of the house, which contributes to close interactions of love between people. Women are the example that children remember. Most times, it is the wife of the house who is the driver and motivator to have the family attend church. Men are not so inclined and choose to stay home or play golf as an example.

On the other hand, the so-called man of the house is exposed to far more sinful opportunities out in the sinful world. In this regard, the man has a harder road to salvation with many more sinful opportunities available to them. Additionally, men view themselves as strong and independent. Manly ego plays a strong influence on the husband. As a result, they view church as a namby-pamby feminine activity. In their minds they do not want to descend into anything that recognizes a higher power, higher than they are and additionally worship. They view this as sacrificing their, "the man and leader of the house."

It is for these reasons that there are significantly less men in Heaven than women. Based on the earthly statistics, only 37% of men reach the Kingdom of God.

Transgenders

57% Make It Back into The Kingdom

Oh, my dearest son, if you asked me this question 20 or 30 years ago, my answer would be very different. However, with Satan's continual invasion of the culture and society in the United States of America, along with sinful policies from the Democrat party, this sexual perversion has been increasingly pronounced. As you know, my dear son, during the teenage years of God's sacred children on earth, they go through a very unstable time in their lives that we call the teenage years. This is where everyone searches desperately for their own identity, discovering who they are, what they enjoy, what they are interested in and what path they might take for the rest of their lives. Teenagers are very susceptible to outside influences of various kinds, some of them good, some of them disastrous.

Because your educational system has been taken over by Satanic people, they have purposely introduced Satanic ideas that diagnose the instability, the natural instability of teenagers trying to find themselves. Many times, a young teenager goes to their counselor and says "I don't feel right. There's something wrong with me. I don't know what it is?" They're in search for themselves as God intended, they might interpret their natural maturing process as not being the right sex. As you know, my dear son, this is 100% not true. Before everyone was born on earth there was an extensive preparation process. It designed the general scope of their coming life experiences and in that process each sacred child chooses if they want to be male or female as part of their life experience.

But now Satan, in working through the educational system, these very naïve and unstable children fall for one of the worst and most disastrous choices they could be influenced into making. Within the atmosphere the government is more and more invading the role of parents in their natural godly functions. The Satanic government makes laws that allow them to interfere in the very heart of the family.

Now, in many places the government confiscates children ripping them away from their family to completely transform the child into the other sex which is mostly man turning into women. This is completely perverse and totally Satanic in every way. These so-called medical people who promote "gender-affirming treatment" are completely guilty of murdering the entire character and inner spiritual being created by God.

Certainly, my dear son, those people who promote this kind of wicked sinful process will never pass to the gates of the Heavenly Kingdom. Anybody, no matter where they are in the chain of influence and implementation of sex changes, always understand where they stand before me in judgment. They will know very well the only place available to them is hell.

The victims of this Satanic program within your educational system are treated mercifully with kindness and love. They are truly victims of a well-thought-out plot in order to destroy their lives, resulting in many committing suicide. But my dear son, it also depends on the scope of their attachment to the idea of changing their agreed-upon gender before being born to earth. There are many who flaunt this in a Satanic manner that they knowingly understand goes against their Heavenly Father's rules for life. Basically, this is a wicked rebellion against their Heavenly Father. Regarding going to the Heavenly Kingdom, these people represent 0%.

Those naive children, unstable, and gullible go through sex change which your government labels and promotes as "gender affirming treatment". These children are really victims of a horrid Satanic plan which serves as one more part of Satan's plan to destroy the American system of godly values and its culture itself. For those who innocently are sold a false bill of goods by evil people, as I said they will be treated with kindness and mercy. It is too soon to have any real statistics on those of God's sacred children who are talked into sex changes. It will depend on how they live the rest of their lives according to the rules of life set forth by your Heavenly Father.

Summary:

I say again, my dearest son, your description of:

<u>*The Democrat Party as The Political Arm of Satan*</u>

<u>*Is Very Correct.*</u>

There is a huge difference in morality and ethics and social responsibility for the health the wellbeing and the safety of the American people between the destructive Democrats and the law-and-order Republicans. <u>*Your country will make a reversal on its current path toward destruction because of our divine intervention with your*</u>

personal angel deflecting the bullet that would have killed Pres. Trump in a matter of minutes. In that instant a sea change of the destiny of your country will begin to happen as I described earlier.

In summary, the Democrats are a tool of Satan, and the Republicans are far Godlier oriented to the best that they can be given the current circumstances. It is for these global reasons that the Democrat percentage of people that go to Heaven is 39%. More than double the entirety of the Democrat party. Remember, the Democrat party has most of its moral and ethical problems in their leadership, not necessarily regular Democrats that vote.

If I were to bunch together the rest of the different religions on earth, the percentage of those people who love Almighty God and their neighbors as themselves, and forgiving toward others, is approximately 23%. Too many of them worship false gods even though on the surface they are good people by secular measurements. Please write down for your readers the summary that you so expertly created to summarize how to get to Heaven.

Summary Statistics

These numbers, as said earlier, are pure and perfect because they come directly from our Lord and Savior, Jesus Christ, directly to me, your author.

Christians	*60%*	*Islam / Muslims*	*6%*
1950s	*2020*		
Priests		*Irreligion*	*1%*
84%	*64%*	*Hinduism*	*18%*
Nuns		*Buddhism*	*27%*
75%	*73%*	*Democrats*	*17%*
Judaism	*43%*	*Democrat Leaders*	*4%*

Republicans	67%	**Agnostics**
Republican leaders	53%	
Males	37%	
Females	63%	
Transgender	57%	
Transgender Promoters	0%	
Atheists	0%	

My last comment on the above information is simple. If you are in one of these groups, you now know the average percentage chance of entering the Heavenly Kingdom. This information is provided to you so that you may conduct heartfelt self-inspection and compare yourself with the rules of life as presented in another part of this book.

As an example, if you identify yourself as a political Democrat, then your average chance of going to Hell is 83%. Why? You believe in abortion and so many other hostile anti-God principles that will certainly condemn you to Hell. Consider this information as a severe warning.

This is all that should be said for now. Your question is very hard-hitting and drills down to the exact truth of things on earth. I know that all your activities are aimed at increasing the number of God's sacred children who will qualify to enter the gates of the Kingdom of Heaven. I deeply thank you for that.

Question: One follow-up question, my dearest Lord: why is the percentage so low from these esteemed leaders of the Catholic Church? I think it may be due to church history, as these numbers were likely given during a time when the Catholic Church had not grown significantly yet.

My dear son, you are indeed a very perceptive person, and yes, you are close to the truth. The number of people that make it into the Heavenly Kingdom is a flexible number across time. For example, the numbers I have provided are current and based on the existence of Christian churches that preach the accurate Christian Bible and teachings. They teach what it is you understand as fundamental Christianity. During ancient times, when the leaders of the church were on earth, what they said was somewhat pessimistic but close to the truth at that time.

Since then, the church has grown enormously, and its effect on the world's population has been very favorable for making people qualify to enter the Kingdom. And as I just said, it has grown to about 30% now.

Question: what happened to the people on earth who lived before you were born as our Lord and Savior? They had no knowledge. I think I know what you're going to say, but I would love to hear it from you, my dear Lord.

Your Father in Heaven is very merciful and fair. It would be very unfair to His sacred children born before I went to earth. They were given a special place in Heaven where they could choose to return to Earth to take the Earth test like everyone else. Or they could choose not to return to Earth for the Earth test again and be among those who made the same choice of remaining in the Heavenly Kingdom. All these people who were born before me were treated with God's loving kindness and given the choice I just described.

This is about as much detail as I wish to get into now, my dear son. For if we were to go further in this line of questions, my answers would become somewhat not understandable due to the complexity of the different situations on earth.

The bottom line is your loving Father in Heaven as you know gives everyone the maximum possibility of entering the Kingdom according to His standards of behavior. We know every one of His sacred children that were born to earth before me. It is easy for us to tell which ones deserve entry into the Kingdom in which ones do not. They will be judged by the same standards as everyone is, with the understanding that they did not know anything about me and were given leeway for that reason. All of this is on an individual basis, just like it is today.

Richard Ferguson

I love you, my dear son, Jesus Christ, Your Lord and Savior, whom you love so very much.

29

Your Author's Commentary and Observations About Life Today and the Real-Life Difficulties of Living a True Christian Life

Life in the 1950s. In Many Ways, It Was Far Better Than Today

I present a summary of my life growing up in Richmond, VA, followed by Chicago, IL, Oakland, California, and Sunnyvale, CA. During this time, there were horrendous changes in life within our beloved United States of America. During my lifetime, before I married my late wife, I observed the social, ethical, and moral standards within our country, and the manner of being, were constantly deteriorating in the United States of America.

During World War II, my mother left her family home in Savannah, IL, where the rest of her family lived. She went to Hastings, Nebraska, where many ammunition plants and others would build tanks, aircraft, and all other forms of war material. Two of my uncles also fought in World War II in the European theater. Both came back with severe mental and emotional issues. During that time, before I was born, our country was overwhelmingly Christian. Everyone went to church on Sunday and prayed before every meal. Yes, dear reader, everyone prayed before every meal that was served. Today, that spiritual practice is almost nonexistent. Many people call this a sign of the times. I call it a sign of moral and spiritual disintegration. Sadly, this trend continues today.

People lived good Christian lives until the 1960s, when the End of Times began. It was not noticeable at first, but as time went on, our country's moral and ethical values started to slip, which continued to slip at a faster and faster rate of change. The End of Times was approaching very quickly.

Growing up, We Moved Around A lot

I was born in 1947 in Richmond, Virginia. Richmond was a tobacco-producing city, and you could say that everyone there was poor and lower-class without much education. The people there still hated those damn Yankees for winning the Civil War. My mother, who was from the Midwest, was considered a damned Yankee, and so was I. As a young boy, I, too, was considered a Northern Yankee. It took the people in the South an exceptionally long time to get over the fact that they lost the Civil War.

Question - Why is it that black people today severely hate white people? Hundreds of thousands of white people were killed and slaughtered by the Confederate army that wanted to continue enslaving black people in the South. They thought that was what God wanted. Yet today, white people are hated terribly when it was and continues to be white people who are promoting the health and well-being of blacks. Through my lived experience, I will tell you that it is because **the Democrat Party Is the Political Arm of Satan. I live in the South. I certainly am quite familiar with hatred against blacks. Yet, in the North, there were job opportunities and more acceptance for black people, but not nearly enough.**

If you want to really understand the Democrat Party, look up accurate books on Lyndon Baines Johnson, the most hateful President of the United States, along with Barack Obama and Joe Biden. I base this very sad judgment comparing these presidents' behavior with our loving Almighty God's 10 commandments and rules for living on earth. If you don't like this previous sentence, I strongly suggest that you consult an objective history book. One of the best objective historians is Victor Davis Hanson. He is unbiased and objective in world events, including especially the history of the

United States of America. [22] His office is at Stanford University in Palo Alto, CA.

The people in Virginia in our Ferguson family were nice enough, but my mom could feel the intense racial tension against her. There was social order, but not a good kind, because black people were considered an underclass and treated poorly. As for me, I thought the blacks who lived with us on the tobacco farm were quite nice and very friendly to me. Of course, I was a very small child, and I may not have been aware of or sensitive to the racial distinctions and attitudes of adults.

There were only a few houses that had indoor plumbing, and almost every house had an outhouse in the back with a deep hole in the ground, for you know what? Everybody either smoked or chewed tobacco. My grandfather loved to chew tobacco and then spit out whatever the hell that awful stuff was. I found out much later that he contracted tongue cancer and died from that. My grandfather Ferguson died of mouth cancer because he really enjoyed chewing tobacco. At least when Grandpa came to visit, he didn't smoke and stink up the House because when you chew tobacco, unfortunately, though, you must spit it out in a spittoon.

By today's standards, people were impoverished, yet at the same time, everyone had a loving attitude toward each other, except for those people who harbored racism within themselves.

At the age of 3 or maybe 5, my parents moved to Chicago with me, making me the only child. We lived on the northwest side in a Polish community. Frankly, I found it pleasant. I remember I could walk anywhere I wanted as a small five-year-old or seven-year-old. However, I did encounter one or two bullies who picked on and shoved me to the ground, and that sort of thing. I never understood that. When I entered kindergarten at St. Tarsisus Catholic school, I walked the 1 mile there without the slightest fear of anything bad happening to me. Even during

---

[22] The Dying Citizen: How Progressive Elites, Tribalism, and Globalization Are Dest 9781541647558 | eBay

the dead of winter, I would walk to and from school. Everybody was safe and secure. You could leave your front and back doors open at night, and nobody would ever come in unannounced. Policeman wore black pants, blue shirts with belts around their waists that containing a 38-caliber six-gun and, on the other side, some handcuffs, and that was it, in addition to the police hats they wore. Their uniform was nothing like the war, like black combat stuff the police wear today.

They were always friendly and smiling at everybody as they walked around, fulfilling their duties to ensure that peace was maintained. They would help the elderly, pushing their shopping carts to their cars and loading the groceries. Crossing the bustling street, Milwaukee Ave, to get to school, if you're interested, it was Milwaukee Avenue, a four-lane street, and a stoplight. I remember the cars would go by quite slowly by today's standards, and everybody obeyed the traffic rules, and I mean everybody. There was a crossing guard for us kids who needed to cross Milwaukee Avenue, and once he put his foot on the pavement, the cars would all stop, even the ones across the street. Nobody ever ran a red light or made an illegal turn that I ever saw. The cars drove slowly down the street. They respected everybody else. Even as a small child back then, going to and from school, I felt very safe.

When I got older, in fifth grade, I became a crossing guard. I wore a white belt and that included a belt that crossed from my left shoulder to my right waist. I had a small sign that I carried that said stop. Whenever I stepped on the street at the stoplight, everybody came to a halt. The cars patiently waited for the very last student to finish crossing the street, and the light turned green before they continued. People in those days were highly respectful of every other person they encountered. Certainly not like today. For those of you who remember the TV show Mayberry RFD, that is what it was like in a big city like Chicago. <u>Now, Chicago has become one of the worst crime-ridden hell-hole cities in our country and the world.</u> The Democrats, in the last four years, purposely opened our southern border and let approximately 15 million illegal aliens into our country. Other countries emptied their jails and prisons and sent them north to us. Now, there has been an explosion of crime where gangs take over large apartment complexes, kicking out the residents.

Going to church was a big deal, and almost everybody went. Women would always wear a hat or, should I say, a cloth-knitted type of head cover, almost always white. There were just as many men as women, and families, big or small, would attend Holy mass. This was during the time only one decade away from World War II. Our country was still recovering. Everybody in the United States was directly affected by World War II in one way or another. It seemed like every family had someone in the military, either in Europe or the Pacific. My Father was in the Army Air Force fixing the radios on B-29 bombers in Guam.

Between 70 to 85 million people were killed in World War II. Back then, our country had 130 million people. 400,000 Americans were killed. Induced disease killed another 419,000. Americans were seriously injured, with many having arms and legs amputated. Additionally, every family in the United States, in one way or another, was directly affected by World War II.

There were food shortages in this country; food was rationed with food stamps. My parents told me a story about when I was a little baby. One day, the only food they had was a little bit of milk and a small hamburger patty, which was all they had on the day before my father got paid. I was two years old, and they gave it to me. My parents didn't eat for two days, maybe three; I don't remember. Yet everybody tried to help everybody else. These were beautiful relationships between sacred children of God, sharing what they had as best they could. If they had something extra, they would give it away to someone who needed it more. The word "extra" does not mean there was an abundance of food. It meant that the food you had exceeded a little bit beyond what was needed to survive to the next paycheck using the food stamps.

Two of my uncles came back from fighting World War II in very bad shape. My uncle Steve was filled with rage and anger, and ultimately, his wife committed suicide. One of my other uncles was a medic in the European theater. This meant part of his job was to, after a ground battle, pick up the body parts and try to sort them together to make a whole body of the same soldier. He was an emotional basket case for many decades. My other two uncles made it back safely and were not as affected the same as the other two I just described.

I tell you this because we are several generations away from the war that determined the world we live in now. The entire Troha family, including me, was quite poor, yet there was a lot of love between everyone. If people like me had not documented the way life was in the 40s, 50s, and early 60s, you will never know how difficult life was in the United States where you live now. <u>Not once did I ever hear anybody complain that somebody else had it better than they did. Everybody pitched in to help everybody else because we all knew we were in the same boat together.</u>

Stop for a moment, please, and think about this. If there were food shortages now in our country. How would people behave? There would be riots and theft beyond our imaginations. Our country has turned into 340 million people who are extremely selfish with a me-first attitude. There would be roving criminal bands attacking people in their homes and stripping away anything they could take regarding food or things that could quickly sell. Our country's moral standards have collapsed.

The loving and moral fiber of our country ever since the 1960s has disintegrated at a rapid and increasingly rapid pace. As I said before, that marked the beginning of the horrific End of Times. I described these details when I co-authored a book with our Blessed Mother Mary. Type my name into your browser, Amazon, or Barnes & Noble, and you will find a few books that I have authored, along with those of members of The Trinity and our Blessed Mother Mary. Our country will have hell to pay and a worse hell to pay for other countries in the world, like those in Europe, especially. The next book I am going to write is a collaboration between our loving, Heavenly, Almighty Father and me. The End of Times is approaching increasingly rapidly. Our Heavenly Father wants to use me as his not only anointed messenger but anointed writer. So, all his secret children on Earth will be warned about what is coming and what they can do to improve themselves and increase their chances of going to heaven after they die. The next book is scheduled for release in late 2025 and serves as a natural follow-up to the one you are currently reading.

Quick summary.

Growing up as a little boy in Chicago was quite pleasant, with one or two exceptions. People were very obedient, and cars obeyed traffic signs, including crosswalks. People regularly went out of their way to help someone else, even if they didn't know that person. Crime was just not an issue where we lived in Northwest Chicago. However, when we moved to Oakland, CA, everything changed. Walking to Mcchesney Junior High School in Glenview Elementary School, I made sure to walk on the right side of the street, avoiding the bullies and punks, as we called them in those days.

Note: After I finish writing this book, our <u>Loving Almighty Father</u> has asked me to write book #4, which is about the End of Times on this earth. About the End of Times that began in the 1960s while President Lyndon Baines Johnson was in the White House. Both are Blessed Mother Mary and suffered through describing what has already happened. But this next book #4 will indeed describe in more detail the suffering coming across the entire earth. This is because 70% of God's sacred children have not followed the rules of life of our loving Heavenly Father.

This next book about the End of Times I will start writing in approximately 6 months. Look for it toward the end of this year 2025.

The most important point is when the 1960s arrived on the calendar crime continually went up, police forces frighteningly overwhelmed and now officers dress like they're going to go into a battle in war. These days you cannot trust anyone anymore and security measures are rampant and make life an extremely hard time for every citizen of our country.

A lot of this is due to the Satanic Democrat Party. There is not one thing that I can remember in the last 20 years that Democrats have done for the benefit of American citizens.

Richard Ferguson

The Effect of The Past on Our Lives Today

Why in the world do I tell you this? It seems like it has nothing to do with advanced theology. It does. During these times of unbelievably bad hardship and suffering in the United States, our country was far closer to Almighty God than it is today. I remember watching Walter Cronkite on the 6 o'clock news each evening when I was growing up. One thing that stands out is that both the Democrat and Republican parties would always openly negotiate things like the Federal budget. It would be for spending the next fiscal year. Representatives from each party would get together and openly negotiate what they wanted. They'd come to compromise agreements that benefited each party but did not give each party everything they wanted. Because they were very fiscally responsible and did not want to spend more than the government took in the way of taxes. I remember Everet Dirkson of the Democrat party being a very nice and honorable man doing the negotiations for His party.

Now, the Democrat Party views Republicans as a vile enemy. President Joe Biden has claimed executive authority, and instead of passing laws that Congress has not agreed to, he uses executive privilege to create White House declarations that have the force and effect of law. The Democrat Party has become a dictatorship and the author of an unbelievable number of lies to deceive God's sacred children and American citizens. Our laws are now rarely voted on by Congress, except for the most consequential ones, at this point. Our federal government is bloated beyond belief. Our two political parties are literally at war with each other and refuse to negotiate for the common good.

The Democrat party is filled with hate. Two days ago, our brain-impaired Pres. Joe Biden gave a speech, and, in the speech, he referred to all the people who are Republicans or want to vote for former president Donald Trump as extremely hateful; they are "garbage." The expression filling his face showed his teeth as if he were going to bite someone while he said, "All those MAGA people need a good kick in their ass." This follows a previous hateful performance of our ex-first lady, Hilary

Clinton, who called anybody that disagrees with her a threat to democracy and other nasty things."

Commentary From Jesus Christ
Lord And Savior Jesus Christ
Sept 28, 2024

My dearest sacred son, what you have just described for the benefit of all the others of your Heavenly Father's children is very true and correct. Every form of life that is ever encountered all originates from our Heavenly Father.

I must emphasize for everyone just how monumentally our Heavenly Father is throughout all His creations. Yes, my dear sacred children, your Heavenly Father has indeed created other creations that have far different purposes than the one all of you are engaged in and living in. These other creations are separate and different and have no bearing whatsoever on life eternally for each and every one of you.

So, my dear sacred son, Richard, has indeed expressed the truth about everyone's existence. It is awful for me and the Holy Spirit to watch His sacred children deny His existence when in fact were it not for the Holy Trinity none of His sacred children would exist. The atheists who deny your Father's existence. Not only is this extremely painful for us within The Trinity but also those people are in effect denying their very own existence when every time they look in a mirror their existence is confirmed.

It is painful for us to continue with the existence of Satan who continues to actively destroy as many of God's sacred children as he can before His time of existence comes to an end. The End of Times our special beloved son, Richard, when he wrote with your Blessed Mother, together they outlined the End of Times, which Richard so accurately and tearfully pointed out began in the 1960s.

I have asked my dearest son Richard to accompany me back to earth during my second coming. People on the earth right now do not know how Holy Richard is but that is also true with my apostles and many others that built my church from scratch. Likewise, my dear sacred children all the books Richard is writing in addition to the Historical Sacred books of your Holy Bible will serve as a foundation. A foundation for the rebuilt Catholic Church after I have come back to reign again on Earth. It makes me extremely pleased that the sacred child you know as Richard will be with me every step of the way.

Although my comments go off the topic of the source of all life, I wanted to include these ever so important thoughts. Because this book is almost at its conclusion before my dear son will start on His next book. A book which addresses in detail basically what Richard would say is, the good the bad and the ugly of the End of Times on Earth. He will expose everyone who has purposely done the work of Satan in destroying God's sacred children in all so many different Satanic ways. After this monumental book, Richard wants to have his 5th major book published. This book is the exploration of our Holy Spirit and the role he plays not only in the creation but also His ongoing role in providing so many things that we take for granted. But without the Holy Spirit life as you know it would not exist and the goals of The Trinity would be very much harder to attain. Your Holy Spirit is the least understood of The Trinity and rightly so. My dearest Richard will be working with the Holy Spirit to create a magnificent book of love, understanding and dedication to the truth and the life that has been made possible by our Heavenly Father.

I love you all ever so very much, Jesus Christ

30

Conclusion:

Congratulations, you have now Learn more about all of existence and the plan that our Heavenly Father has for everyone of His sacred children in the objective reality we call life. All the information that is contained in this book is either directly authored by our Holy Trinity and our Blessed Mother Mary or directly approved.

This is nothing like our magnificent sacred Bible because most of it is written directly from members of our Trinity and Blessed Mother Mary. I am Our Holy Father's anointed messenger. During the writing of this book, I have been told many times that He is very pleased with what is written herein. Unlike our Holy Bible, this book is written one step beyond being inspired by God. There are no interpretations of Godly information. It is presented directly from our Trinity and our Blessed Mother Mary.

Unlike our Holy Bible, the contents of this book do not rely on more than 66 different authors that provide God's sacred children with information about our objective existence within God's creation. Again, all information comes directly from the words spoken by members of The Trinity and Blessed Mother Mary. What they say directly to me is instantly transcribed to a Microsoft Word file exactly as I hear it from them. They are the words that are printed within this book.

If you take heart to the information provided in this book regarding how to get back into heaven, you will never fail in returning to our heavenly kingdom from where we all came from.

I so very much look forward to seeing all of you within the heavenly kingdom as time comes to go back home with our Heavenly Father.

Blessings and Love, Your Author, Richard

APPENDIX 1

Special Section

This is published so you can understand in detail just how lovingly close the Holy Trinity really is to each of us, every moment of every day of our lives.

The Assassination Attempt of Now President Donald J. Trump

I have included this last section to demonstrate to you just how close Almighty God is to each of us every moment of every day of our lives while we're on Earth. Below is a message from our Lord and Savior Jesus Christ to me personally on the Sunday after the assassination attempt of our presidential candidate, Donald Trump, in Butler, PA.

I want you to focus on a few very powerful points about this assassination attempt.

1. The Holy Trinity knew about this assassination attempt well before it came to fruition.

2. They knew exactly all the people who were directly involved; all 12 are Democrats. Some of their names are listed in the message from Jesus to give you an idea of the detailed information we have.

3. Our Lord and Savior Jesus Christ said that this assassination attempt, if successful, would have changed the entire trajectory of our country all for the bad.

4. **One of my personal protective archangels is the one that deflected the bullet from Donald Trump's skull into the upper part of his ear so it would produce blood, proving it was an assassination attempt.** Otherwise, Democrats would instantly claim there was no assassination attempt, and it was just staged by the Republicans.

5. Not only did one of my Angels save the life of Donald Trump, but he also saved the entire future of our country. Within this message from Jesus, we are told why and what would have happened if he was really killed.

The Assassination Attempt of President Donald Trump in Butler, PA. This Assassination Attempt Was Planned By

12 Democrat Leaders and Appointees.

While writing this book, a shocking event occurred. It was when there was an assassination attempt against the life of President Donald Trump at a political rally in Butler, PA. Additionally, there was a second assassination attempt two months later. Lastly, we have recent information that Iran has hired more assassins to kill now President-elect Donald Trump. This is a clear act of war against our country.

I feel it important to include what happened at the rally where President Donald Trump spoke for about three minutes before shots rang out. He was hit on the right side of His head before he fell to the floor. It is especially important that you keep in mind a few things that all came together in a flash of time.

1. The Holy Trinity knew in advance that this was going to happen.

2. Normally, stated by Jesus Christ, The Trinity would not interfere with ongoing human events. But this time, it was incredibly special because this assassination attempt was hatched by only 12 people in high-up positions within the Democrat Party.

Stated by Jesus Christ, had they let this assassination attempt succeed, the United States of America would end up down a road of painful grinding into nothingness. A country where all its citizens would experience great suffering and agony at the hands of just a very few people in the Democrat Party. Over the last few years, I have stated many times that <u>The Democrat Party is the Political Arm of Satan!</u>

3. <u>The Trinity decided to use one of my two very powerful angelic beings that are here to protect me and members of my family from the constant attacks we experience from Satan.</u>

4. Perhaps, this is hard for you to believe, but one of my Angels went to Butler, PA. in the blink of an eye and deflected the bullet from the lower part of President Trump's skull. If my personal angel not done this, the bullet would have killed President Trump in a very few minutes.

5. Yes, my protective angels are that powerful and that precise. Remember, please, every book I write and everything I say is immensely hated by Satan and his demons. It is my personal belief that without them, I would have died a long time ago. I forget if I included this next story in this book or not. But when I was in my 30s, Satan personally attacked me on three separate occasions. He interrupted me in the middle of the night and screamed at me these words, "**I will get you; I will get you; I will get you!**" The most complete story about these Satanic attacks can be found in my first book titled: "God's **Grand Design of All Creation for Your Redemption."**

I was completely shocked when I asked our Lord and Savior, Jesus Christ, what percentage of the Democrat Party leaders made their way back into the Heavenly Kingdom. His answer is pure and perfect because Jesus Christ is God. He is the ultimate speaker of complete truth. When he told me that only 3% to 4% of those people in Democrat Party leadership positions make their way back into the Heavenly Kingdom, I was just shocked to think it was so low. After pondering it for a while and reflecting on the statements made by the Biden administration, among others, I came to realize, as I often do, that Jesus is perfectly correct.

Additionally, after reading the below message from Jesus, the awful percentages of Democrat Party leaders that make their way back into the Heavenly Kingdom will now make a lot more sense. As I have said many times before, <u>The Democrat party is indeed "The Political Arm of Satan" in our country today.</u> If you doubt what I say, look at their policies and focus on the Democrat policies for the last four years. Compare those with Christian values and ethics. You will find as I did that Democrat policies go against Christian teachings 90% of the time if not 100 per cent.

If you are a Christian, there is absolutely no way you can vote Democrat. There is just one glaring point on this subject. Abortion! After that, there is a blizzard of more reasons never to vote Democrat.

What Jesus Told Me About the Very Next Day After the Assassination Attempt

Next is my conversation with our Lord and Savior, Jesus Christ, on the day after the attempted assassination that took place the evening before. Our conversation also includes a few other things that you will find remarkably interesting.

Lord Jesus speaks to me, His Anointed Messenger, Regarding The Donald Trump Assassination Attempt
July 14, 6:00 PM.

My dearest son Richard, I wanted to explain a few things to you about the recent events yesterday and today in your country, America. Yesterday, there was a legitimate and intentional attack against your presidential candidate, Donald Trump. Your government knew about this coming attack, and they turned their backs on what they knew was going to happen. This is one of your government's tactics. To manipulate the people, your Father's sacred children, who live there.

The Democrat Party has actively and vigorously promoted so many heinous sins against your Heavenly Father. And what you said about the Democrat Party as my mother has said is that you are entirely correct when you label them as the "The Political Arm of Satan."

The fact a rooftop gunman with the clear view towards Trump, when he was speaking was allowed to happen is proof that your government purposely dropped the ball. This kind of thing to happen with what your government calls, "Reasonable Deniability."

Yesterday, I mentioned, my dear son, one of your personal angels instantly modified the trajectory of the one bullet. The bullet that would have otherwise struck Donald Trump at the base of His neck on the right side higher into the cranial area. It would have killed Him in a few minutes. But your angel deflected that bullet, so it penetrated the top of His right ear as everyone knows now. What they do not know is that divine intervention saved literally your entire country from a horrific, grinding, and painful end of its history.

My dear son, normally, we do not interfere with political events or the History of nations. This is because all of that is a product of the gift of free will that your Father has bestowed upon all His sacred children on earth. But in this case, there were only a few very guilty people high up in your government. These including your president Joe Biden and others you know about like Hillary Clinton and a few others that gave secret orders to the Secret Police that you have posing as protectors of Mr. Trump.

(The following text was told to me on July 14, 2024, the day after the assassination attempt and long before the election in November)

Donald Trump will win the coming election in a huge landslide which will shift the political scene entirely in favor of the foundational principles, the Godly foundational principles, that your country was founded upon. Mr. Trump, after he is in office, there will be many investigations to ferret out the criminals that have been so well entrenched in ever so many of your government branches.

The Communist sympathizers within your country will largely stop shouting so loudly, and many of them will question what their political beliefs were.

Our Father has seen the change of heart of many citizens of the United States!

Your Almighty Father wants to give your country another chance

to avoid all the terrors and horrors of the End of Times, as my Mother has described to you in great detail!

Europe, however, will continue to burn because of all the Muslims they allowed into their countries. As you know, my dear son, and have said many times, <u>Islam is the religion of Satan</u>. Of this there is no doubt about anybody that wishes to think about it in an objective manner. Both of us, you're Blessed Mother and I, are so happy that your second major book is now in the publisher's hands. Advantage will do a very good job for you. Your friend and colleague, Mike, will do everything properly. The next two or three booklets which you plan on publishing in the next three or four months are wonderful and please continue with that. Then I am looking forward to working with you and speaking together like we did on the first book to produce the third major book for people, which is how to get back into Heaven. And I know you're already thinking about the contents. As always, I will be at your side, along with your Blessed Mother.

I know you have a question in mind. Please articulate it, and I will answer.

Question: Thank you, dear Lord. Is there any one phenomenon or event that our Heavenly Father and You and the Spirit that influenced you to decide that the United States would be given a second chance?

Answer: There were several things, my dear son. We could see within the hearts of ever so many millions of people in the United States that they were rejecting more and more and more of the Communist Manifesto being perpetrated on them.

In your country, more and more people are taking action to support the fundamental principles upon which your country was founded, which, as we all know is based upon the rules of life set forth by your Heavenly Father.

And we also knew how to release that beautiful energy into the social and cultural dimension of your country; it needed a spark of some kind. A spark which would ignite the pent-up passions and desires of your people for Almighty God. Desire to be expressed within your society and take it away from the Marxist and Communist people that have thrived all too long in your culture and in your country.

It is now that, as you would say, my dear son, the worm has turned. In this case, for the much, much better.

Question: My dearest Lord Jesus, would you feel it appropriate to name others who conspired in this assassination attempt, please?

Answer: *of course, my dear son. The other names include Kamala Harris., the director of the FBI., the local Secret Service manager and the head of the Secret Service for the whole country. The local police officers and others that live in that small town knew nothing about this. It was the top people in the Secret Service that hatched this plan and ordered the higher ups in that organization in collusion with the FBI to create this assassination attempt.*

<u>*In short there were approximately 12 people, all Democrats and Democrat appointees, who conspired to kill President Trump.*</u>

Of course, my dear son, the head of the FBI and one of his lieutenants were also directly involved. They then passed orders down their command hierarchy for some of their people not to do certain things that created the hole for the assassin to do his killing.

But, my dearest son, your Father and I decided to use one of your angels that protect you to deflect the bullet just enough to wound your next president very slightly. We knew this was necessary to demonstrate to your entire country the <u>vile Satanic nature of the Democrat party.</u> There will be a flushing out of all the criminals that have infected the police, security forces and your military forces in the coming few years. This will take time because as you always say, dearest son, it takes only a little explosive to blow up a building but a lot of time and effort to rebuild it again.

God's sacred children in your country that believe in the Holy Trinity and live according to what your Heavenly Father has put forth deserve a second chance. Along with a further chance to spread His Holy words of redemption, which is precisely what is contained in those books you have already written and those still to come. And as you know, my dearest of sons, you and your family are protected in the same manner that Pres. Trump has been and will continue to be.

I love you ever so much, my dearest son.

Thank you, my dearest Lord, and Savior Jesus Christ. I love you too!

An In-Depth Analysis of What Our Lord and Savior Jesus Just Said:

1. There was a minimum of 12 Democrats within our government who knew ahead of time that the assassination attempt would take place.
2. Democrats manipulated things to be able to plead "reasonable deniability."
3. As a general long-lasting note, the Democrat party has strongly promoted so many heinous sins against our Heavenly Father both now and in the past.
4. The Democrat party of today is indeed **The Political Arm of Satan in Our Country. Our Lord and Savior Agrees with This Completely**
5. The Secret Service purposely left that rooftop open, which had a clear view of Pres. Donald Trump for his assassination.
6. It was one of my personal archangels that instantly deflected the bullet in such a manner that it was allowed to slightly injure President Trump. I have two powerful angels that protect me from Satan. Because of my importance in bringing forth to all of God's sacred children His messages of love, of peace, of understanding to His creations. To do this in a far deeper way that if a person reads what is said in the books, I write they will make it back into the Heavenly Kingdom. My personal protective angels are Saint Gabriel and Saint Michael. And yes, my dear sacred children of God, their names are within our Blessed Holy Bible.

7. Understand that angels can and do, on rare occasions, come into the physical realm to fulfill the will of our Almighty Father and our Lord and Savior, Jesus Christ. Scientists would call this trans-dimensional.

8. If Donald Trump were assassinated on that day in Butler, Pennsylvania, the Democrats would retain power. Our country would irrevocably march down a horrific destructive path that would wipe out all Christians and Christian teachings of our Holy Father. Our country would become a cesspool of horrific sin, very much like Sodom and Gomorrah. As I write this for you today, our beloved United States is already on its way to copy Sodom and Gomorrah exactly. Justice would be a thing of the past, and Christians would indeed have to go underground to celebrate Holy Mass. Christians will be killed on site, and so on. The United States of America will have long passed away into the dustbin of History because Satan will become the ruler of the world. The possession of this book that you are reading will become so illegal that if you are found with this book, you will be executed on the spot. Of course, that will also apply to all Biblical literature.

9. *This divine intervention is an exceedingly rare event because we within The Trinity do not interfere with the free will of our sacred children on earth. However, in this case, your Heavenly Father has seen a beautiful uprising of many people within the United States. People who are turning more and more toward our loving Father in their hearts within themselves and are more and more attracted to the truth of His creations and His rules for life. Therefore, we in The Trinity felt that since there are only a very few horrifically Satanic people in the leadership of the Democrat party that promoted this heinous sin against Pres. Trump, we decided to save your country from oblivion at the hands of the Democrat party leadership. It is not an understatement to say that we saved the entire future of your country from oblivion at the hands of a few Satanic individuals at the top of your Democrat party. Jesus Christ August 2024*

10. Donald Trump will win the next election for president. He will win in a landslide, and he will take great measures to undo the

horrific damage the Democrat party has done to your country starting on January 5, 2025.

11. The Democrat party will continue in their Satanic ways, and they will do anything and everything to block what President Trump will do to save our nation from the claws of Satan. Remember, I am a prime target of Satan and was directly attacked by Satan personally three times in the middle of the night. His red eyes came within 18 inches from my face.

12. **After the election, the communist sympathizers and pure communist political leaders inside your government will largely stop shouting so loudly, and some of them will start questioning what their personal political beliefs are.**

13. Make sure you understand that what has been done for your country is a second chance to grow closer to your Heavenly Father. Your country has committed horrific sins against our Father in so many ways. The first that comes to mind is abortion, which is the most heinous and Satanic act anybody can possibly do. Over 70 million sacred children of God have had their physical bodies ripped apart in the name of a woman's right to choose. Nobody on earth has the right to kill a developing sacred child of our Heavenly Father. Those that do are condemning themselves to hell.

14. So, the United States of America has been granted a second chance to lift your country to Godly and sacred behavioral standards. Again, I say this is a second chance. It is not a pardon by any means. Our country will not avoid all the terrors and heartaches along with pain, suffering, and death. Rather, we will experience a diluted part of the End of Times, and yes, there will still be terror, heartache, pain, and suffering within our country. But again, it will not be to the horrific extent that will exist in the rest of the world, for example, within Europe. As I write this, Europe is well on its way toward self-destruction. This means for us a lot of hard work in the name of Almighty God. The Trinity wants so very much for everyone to understand this choice and the great second chance that has been given unto you.

15. *Europe, on the other hand, will burn itself into oblivion because of all the Muslim people they allowed into their countries. As this*

is written by the hands of my anointed messenger, you are already going down into a hellish existence. This will continue as was described by your author. That is when he published a magnificent book with your Blessed Mother Mary that describes in detail the End of Times in the horrific suffering that is coming to that land of self-condemnation.

16. **Islam is, indeed, "the religion of Satan."** Yes, my dear sacred children of our Almighty Father, Islam is indeed the religion of Satan. A tree can be known by its fruits, and if you are interested enough, just look at the fruits Islam is born. It is nothing more than death, suffering, Satanic control over everyone's lives, and the hellish domination of every person not only in their actions but in their thoughts. **Satan rules by hate and fear**. This is completely demonstrated by everything Islam has ever touched on earth.

My suggestion to people in political power in your country is that they take strong and definitive action to deport every Muslim that has entered your country in the last five or more years. The immigration the Democrat party allowed into your country will go an exceedingly long way in destroying everything accomplished for the benefit of your Father's sacred children. It is the Democrat party that wants to see this happen. Both Islam and the Democrat party have the same goal, which is to destroy the United States of America because it was founded on Judeo-Christian ethics and principles and morality.

These people view your country as the enemy of Satan, and therefore, the Democrat party wants to destroy it by any means possible. This is why Barack Obama refused to salute the flag when the band played the Star-Spangled Banner at a football game. Barack Obama, no matter what you think, planted the most destructive and evil seeds within our society with his identity politics policy.

Identity politics simply means there is a different set of laws for Obama's favored races and far stricter laws for whites or non-color people. Blacks or people of color are given special favors only because they are of color. Tight laws are for all others. Even today, the Democrat candidates for president in this year, 2020 and 24, have proposed great financial benefits to black people only because they are black! Yet our corrupt elites in charge of our news media have never once accused the Democrat Party of racism, which is exactly what this is. One disastrous example is the concept that everyone can do any job, no matter what their skill set or IQ, or aptitude, to perform tasks for specific jobs.

DEI is a horrific manifestation of this time bomb policy. I hold a commercial pilot's license and other licenses. More than 2,000 hours of flight experience. I was a flight instructor for a time as well. I encountered a few people who were just NOT capable of being a safe pilot, no matter how much training they were given. Now, there are many deadly flight incidents where incompetent DEI pilots caused fatal accidents that killed so many innocent passengers. But you will be very hard-pressed to see accurate news articles that accurately place the DEI pilot to blame. This does not even count the near misses saved at the last second by the other experienced captain.

Our completely corrupt news media is also a tool of Satan. They accomplish this by complete hatred against anything that is of our Loving, Almighty Father. They lie terribly. They ignore anything that is for the good of God's sacred children on earth. They invent fake negative stories against anything positive and Godly within our beloved country.

It was designed to pit one group of people against another. This is exactly the opposite of the will of our Heavenly Father. I refer to the pages of this book where I cover the probabilities of people going to Heaven based on their allegiance to various kinds of groups. People who are leaders in the Democrat Party only have about a 6% chance of entering the majestic gate of Heaven. Why? They love Satan way too much!

At this point, the Democrat Party are professional racists in every way you can think of if you care to be objective about things. During this 2024 presidential election, the horrific hatred the Democrat Party shows fort Trump is absolutely horrifying. As this is written now, Kamala Harris has been accusing former President

Donald Trump of being a fascist. She also is accusing him of admiring Hitler from World War II.

This is Satanic at its very core. Yet, as was foretold in the Bible thousands of years ago, the Antichrist will bring death, destruction, chaos and confusion into society. He will do this through his suave and smooth speeches and giving the people something that seems good but at its core brings nothing more than death and destruction to the people of God.

My dear sacred children of Almighty God, this is an awful sad point for me right now as a writer because this book is now finished. I hope and pray I'll do all the demanding work of not only mine, but all the other people involved in the printing, editing, and distribution of this book that they too are prayed for. As mentioned earlier, at the direct request of our Heavenly Father, I have changed the next book from an exploration of our Holy Spirit. Instead, I will investigate as Jesus said, "the good, the bad, and the ugly regarding the End of Times, which is now in its 60th year." I will certainly name names and bring forth a lot of the hidden treachery that has been across the world and in our country. Even the Democrat Party itself. Continue to realize that the End of Times will be a long and drawn-out period of suffering and agony for God's sacred children on Earth. For now, always remember that **it is truly the Democrat Party in the United States that is the political arm of Satan.** The proof of this will continue to become more and more clear and astonishing.

God's blessings and love to all, Richard
Our Heavenly Father's Anointed Messenger

APPENDIX 2

God's Sacred Children's Health and Healing

What Healing Really Is. Described By Jesus Christ

He said that *"the miracle of healing is really a very accelerated process of the body's normal healing. Each of us has built into our physical bodies an immensely complex immunological system that kills disease. Healing is what it means. It kills off that which would terminate life. In your case, my dear son, it was the will of your Father to extend your life, and so we did by simply greatly amplifying your natural healing processes within your body. The treatment you got from your doctor certainly helped a great deal. Also, your doctors were exceptionally good at what they did."*

Why do I tell you this since it seems so out of place? It is because this book contains real-life Spiritual events. Everyone must remember that the physical realm overlaps greatly with the spiritual realm. In fact, the physical realm is contained within the spiritual realm. There will come a time when the physical realm will no longer exist because it is no longer needed within God's plan with his sacred children.

My healing was a true and purposeful spiritual event given to me by The Trinity itself. Nothing in this book is theoretical or based on someone's third-hand story or a vision they had. No! All communications that I have had with Almighty God are for certain very real events that happened exactly as presented. All events that are personal in nature are also real-life things that happened. All the communications that you see within this book are the exact words that were communicated to me by Jesus Christ and other members of The Trinity, along with Blessed Mother Mary.

If anybody says something different, what they say is born out of misunderstandings on their part or other negative motivations.

Most people believe that we are here on earth and God is out "there" somewhere in Heaven. This is not the case. There is no spatial difference between God and us His sacred children. God is omnipresent meaning that our Almighty Father is right here on earth with us right now. He is so close to every one of His children that we can speak to Him any time we wish. Remember what Biblical Scripture says about this point. God knows how many hairs you have on your head. Do not be afraid. You are worth more than many small birds.[23] Read the upcoming story about being with God related to this very book.

Please remember:

I Am the Only Sacred Child of God that Has Been Gifted By Our Heavenly Father to Not Only Speak with Him but Also Write Down His Words for The Benefit of All His Sacred Children on Earth. I refer you to the first page of all my books.

The Fatal Sickness of My Late Wife

My wife, about 25 years ago, developed fatal cancer. Through my prayers, however, our Heavenly Father extended her life from the normal 18 months that her cancer would last to five years. During those five years, I devoted 100% of my time, attention, and love to my wife, taking care of her every minute of every day. I completely ignored myself and any health maintenance that would normally be required at my age. Unknown to me, I was developing a profoundly serious situation of prostate cancer. This cancer was so far gone it was fatal by the time I went to a doctor.

About seven or eight years after the death of my late wife, I met a most wonderful woman that I will spend the rest of my happy life with. My dear fiancé who was a professor of theology at Santo Tomas University in Manila, Philippines, kept bugging me to get a physical exam from a

---

[23] Luke 12:7 New Life Version

doctor. No man likes going to the doctor, including me. But I relented. Good thing I did. My PSA score was extremely high, way into the fatal region.

I had no symptoms, but it was already fatal when discovered. I did get highly aggressive radiation and chemical treatments Both my doctors and the radiation doctor told me "Do not get near any small children." Basically, my midsection must have glowed in the dark. I was cured completely because of direct divine intervention on my behalf. My urologist emphasized this to me.

Years later, God our Loving Father told me it "*was His will that I will survive*." I will tell you a sacred secret that Jesus Christ said to me recently. Please remember this for your own education about how close our Heavenly Father is to every one of us.

This book is a book of real-life Spiritual events that occurred. The words from our Lord and Savior Jesus Christ, our Heavenly Father, and our Blessed Mother Mary were all spoken to me very clearly in plain American English. It had to be this way so the messages of The Trinity and Mother Mary would shine with their divine brilliance in truth for the benefit of all our Heavenly Father's sacred children on earth. In other words**, YOU!**

If you have a copy of this book in your hands, consider yourself extremely lucky because the earth entered the End of Times in the 1960s. The times ahead for the people on Earth will get harder and harder and more calamitous as time goes on. All of this is outlined in detail in the second book I have published with our Blessed Mother Mary. Its title is "God's **Grand Design, Mother Mary Speaks, Her Apparitions, The End of Times. "One** of the horrifying truths that is described in detail in this second book is the fact that our Pope Francis is indeed the Antichrist. Much proof is provided. **It is undeniable proof that Satan lives in the Vatican.** I got sick to my stomach and depressed several times while writing what our Blessed Mother described as what would happen during the End of Times.

Societies and Cultures Are Far Sicker Than I Ever Was.

I have said in my other writings in addition to this book, the End of Times was prophesied in many books of Biblical literature. It started worldwide in the 1960s.

The following book will be exclusively written by our Heavenly Father and me. We will be co-authors. We will concentrate on the many details worldwide about the End of Times before our Lord and savior Jesus Christ returns to Earth. Most of us think that the End of Times automatically is for The United States only. Not true, it is a worldwide disaster due to all the horrible levels of sin in this world. Pardon the pun, but that it will be of Biblical proportions.

If you observe worldwide events today, you will see that more and more countries are disintegrating at one rate or another toward horrific social unrest and war. There already is mounting frequency of natural disasters. This will only increase into unimaginable. This also includes great natural disasters, including earthquakes, floods, famines, and other horrible disasters that our planet is not at all prepared for. England, Canada, and France are quickly disintegrating right now because their government did NOT know one simple fact. Adherence to the Christian and godly rules of our existence on Earth must be obeyed otherwise terrible things happen to all the people and individually.

A final note about the End of Times coming soon, having started in the 1960s, our Lord and savior Jesus Christ has stated He wants me to accompany Him during his return to Earth. I was completely surprised when He told me this a few months ago. Of course, I said YES! I certainly will!

APPENDIX 3

Book #4 To Come

Almighty God and I Will Co-Author Book #4

Note: Sometime earlier in this book, I mentioned that my next book, book #4, will be totally dedicated to understanding all the details of our Holy Spirit. It is fascinating! However, our Heavenly Father has asked me to postpone writing that book and instead write a book that addresses the ever-increasing evil in our world today. In the book that our Blessed Mother Mary and I wrote earlier, substantial space was given to The End of Times. But that book was not comprehensive regarding the End of Times. Most of us will live through the End of Times.

Book #4 will be comprehensive, covering all areas of the Earth. In the meantime, please disregard TV shows and YouTube videos, as they hold no authority whatsoever. Book #4 will indeed be written by Almighty God Himself as the primary source, and I will play a secondary role in the writing. I estimate that Book #4, regarding the moral condition of the Earth, will be available on various literary websites in August-September 2025.

The book our Heavenly Father and I will write will be comprehensive and span many, many years on Earth. In the next book, it will be our Heavenly Father and I who will co-author Book Number 4. I don't have a title for it right now, but it will directly address the ongoing disintegration of Planet Earth. It will examine how punishments will be related to each section of Earth and its sinful historical ways. And timewise, it will probably end with the second coming of our Lord and Savior, Jesus Christ. My direct involvement with our Holy Trinity will continue eternally beyond my death, and Jesus has asked me to be with Him during His second coming. I like that.

Since Mother Mary and I wrote the book about her apparitions and the End of Times, Jesus Christ told me I would be better off with my family. That we should move from the area where I currently live to a smaller community in the northern part of the San Joaquin Valley of California. That is what I will do. As I have mentioned before, <u>we are now living in the End of Times</u>. We entered the End of Times in the early 1960's. It was peaceful living in our country back then. However, Lyndon Baines Johnson, our Democrat president, got us into the Vietnam War in 1966. In 1975, the war ended after 3.95 million of God's sacred children were killed. I want to throw up!

I lived in the 1960s as a child growing up. People were friendly. When I crossed the street to get to the school, the cars were very friendly in that they never came close to the crosswalk, and none of them speeded. People were law-abiding. Police officers only wore dark pants, a blue shirt, an official hat, a belt with a .38 caliber revolver, and a pair of handcuffs. That was it. People looked up to the police as protectors of their safety and security. Over the last 50 years or so, our society has undergone a significant decline. When my children went to school, they could have walked, but in the 1970s and 1980s, things had already disintegrated in our society. Disintegrated to the point where we drove them to school and picked them up. Everywhere, crime took hold with gang activity.

Every day, every week, every month, and every year that passes, there will be constant increases in violence, dishonesty, and natural disasters beyond anything that has ever happened before on Earth. Dormant volcanoes will come to life. One volcano is already breaching the surface of the Pacific Ocean about halfway between San Francisco and Tokyo. Weather patterns will change entirely, and floods of a great magnitude we have never heard of before will terrorize the earth, along with earthquakes in places where there were none before. If you live in a flood-prone area, get out and move to higher ground. There will be terrible floods as the result of torrential rains in places that have never experienced that before.

Now, in the 2020s, our former Democrat president Joe Biden and Vice President Harris opened up our southern border to uncountable violent gangs, drug dealers, and horrifically slave traders of small children. This is horrifically disgusting and illegal. Additionally, this has led to significant local increases in crime statistics. So far, our country has admitted to spending $80 billion dollars to support these criminals and illegal aliens. There are so many ugly stories from what the Democrat party has done to our beloved United States of America.

As Jesus Christ told me recently, the End of Times is here and now and will only get worse. Our beloved United States of America. However, we will not experience the full brunt of the End of Times. Rather we will experience a watered down reduced End of Times and its associated suffering. However, make no mistake. It will be awful and rotten. It's just that, comparing hurricanes, our country will experience 120 mile-per-hour winds, whereas the rest of the world, because of them ignoring our Heavenly Father, will experience 170 or 180 mile-per-hour winds. This is frightening for me. Our Heavenly Father has noticed within our people that they are moving closer to Him than before. Sadly, however, all of Europe will burn.

Food shortages will increase dramatically and become scarce, along with medical supplies to treat the people living on Earth. The death rate will increase horribly. There will be shortages of every consumable globally, and fuel for our cars will be extremely difficult to get hold of at horrifically high prices. Basic survival will be the goal of every family on earth. There will come a time when the living will indeed envy the dead. Suffering will increase horribly. The above description is not the plot for a Hollywood scare movie; rather, it will play out in real life.

Why will all of this happen? Our Holy Bible has prophesied that what we are experiencing now is something Christians have known about for thousands of years. Like all human things, it is the propensity of God's sacred children on earth not to believe biblical stuff unless it is knocking on their heads.

Richard Ferguson

www.ingramcontent.com/pod-product-compliance
Lightning Source LLC
Chambersburg PA
CBHW060834190426
43197CB00039B/2594